# These Words Are Written

## Devotions on the Gospel of John

Stephen Helwig

NORTHWESTERN PUBLISHING HOUSE

Milwaukee, Wisconsin

Northwestern Publishing House
N16W23379 Stone Ridge Dr., Waukesha, WI 53188
www.nph.net
© 2024 Northwestern Publishing House
Published 2024
Printed in the United States of America
ISBN 978-0-8100-3162-3
ISBN 978-0-8100-3163-0 (e-book)

24  25  26  27  28  29  30  31  32  33       10   9   8   7   6   5   4   3   2   1

# Preface

In the gospel of John, we find some of the most well-known and well-loved passages in all of Scripture. "Look! The Lamb of God, who takes away the sin of the world!" (John 1:29). "For God so loved the world that he gave his only-begotten Son, that whoever believes in him shall not perish, but have eternal life" (John 3:16). "I am the resurrection and the life. Whoever believes in me will live, even if he dies. And whoever lives and believes in me will never perish" (John 11:25,26).

The gospel of John also contains some of the most familiar and some of the most often shared Bible stories in all of Scripture. Jesus turning water into wine at the wedding in Cana. Jesus feeding the five thousand with five loaves of bread and two small fish. Jesus washing his disciples' feet in the upper room the night before his death. Peter and John racing to the tomb on Easter morning only to find it empty. At that same tomb, Mary Magdalene actually thinking that Jesus was the gardener!

It is in John's gospel that Jesus shares and teaches and explains things that, quite simply, are difficult for us to understand logically in our minds but are so important for us to believe by faith in our hearts. Jesus is the Son of God—the Word—through whom all things were created, but he is also the Son of Man—the Word that became flesh—who made his dwelling among us (John chapter 1). Jesus talked about the need for people to eat his flesh and drink his blood, but, in the context, he wasn't even talking about the Lord's Supper (John chapter 6)! Jesus claimed that he and the Father are one (John chapter 10). He also claimed that whoever has seen him has seen the Father (John chapter 14).

And yet, all of it—each chapter, each verse, each word; the well-known and the unfamiliar, the simple and the difficult, the Bible stories and the discourses, the parables and the miracles—all of it was written so that "you may believe that Jesus is the Christ, the Son of God, and that by believing you may have life in his name" (John 20:31). May the Holy Spirit bless you and your faith to that end as you read this book of devotions based on the gospel of John.

# The Word

## John 1:1-3

*In the beginning was the Word, and the Word was with God, and the Word was God. He was with God in the beginning. Through him everything was made, and without him not one thing was made that has been made.*

The opening words of John's gospel—"In the beginning"— take us back to the opening words of the Old Testament book of Genesis and the creation account where God said, " 'Let there be light,' and there was light" (Genesis 1:3).

The Word that John refers to in the opening verse of his gospel is not the written Word of God; it's not the Bible; it's not the Scriptures. The Word that John refers to in the opening verse of his gospel is God himself. In the verses that follow, John will make it clear to us that this Word, who is God, is none other than Jesus Christ, the Son of God who took on human flesh. So what do we learn about the Word—about Jesus Christ, about the Son of God— who took on human flesh in the opening verses of John's gospel?

We learn that Jesus is eternal, that he has no beginning and no end; he was there "in the beginning" as only God was. In fact, he was actually there before the beginning. We also learn that not only was Jesus with God but he actually is God. Note the unique relationship between the Father and the Son; there is only one God, yet he reveals himself in three persons—God the Father, God the Son, and God the Holy Spirit. Finally, we learn that the eternal Son of God, Jesus Christ, the Word who became flesh, was active in creation. Without him, nothing has been made; by him, all things were made.

Already from the start of John's gospel, we see the eternal God—the almighty God, the Son of God, Jesus Christ, the one who was active in the creation of the world—coming to the aid and help of sinful human beings. We see him coming to our aid! And all this he, the Word, would do by becoming "flesh" and making his dwelling "among us" (John 1:14). So as we set out to read John's gospel together, let us never forget that Jesus is the Word. He came to fulfill God's gospel promises; in fact, Jesus is the gospel—in him and in him alone we have the good news of our salvation.

*Holy Spirit, I thank you for the written Word of God that makes me wise for salvation through faith in Christ, the Word made flesh. Amen.*

---

## Life and Light

### John 1:4,5

> *In him was life, and the life was the light of mankind. The light is shining in the darkness, and the darkness has not overcome it.*

The Word is God, and the Word was active in creation—all things were created through him. We heard that in the opening verses of John's gospel.

Notice how John states that in these verses. "In him"—the Word—"was life." The Word brought life to the world. Miraculously speaking, the Word did that by his almighty power. Practically speaking, the Word did that by giving light to his creation. Notice how a plant thrives in the proper light, how it leans and grows toward a sunny window and away from the darkness of the rest of the room. That plant would quickly die if it was locked in a dark closet—cut off from the light.

But is that all we have here? Is all we have here the Word bringing both life and light to his creation? Thankfully, we have so much more! Thankfully, the Word has also brought us spiritual life through the light of the Word. Dead in sin, trapped in a dark closet of unbelief, not only could we not see the light but we had no life spiritually. We couldn't come to the light. We couldn't release ourselves from that dark spiritual closet (prison) of unbelief, but the life that is the light of men could—and did!

In him, we have life. In him, we have faith. In him, we have forgiveness. In him, we have hope. In him, we have eternal life. And all this through the Word!

*Holy Spirit, keep me seated in the sunny window of the light of Christ, rooted in his Word, growing in his grace, and producing fruit. Amen.*

---

## The Witness

### John 1:6-9

*There was a man, sent from God, whose name was John. He came as an eyewitness to testify about the light so that everyone would believe through him. He was not the light, but he came to testify about the light. The real light that shines on everyone was coming into the world.*

God had promised that the seed of the woman would crush the serpent's head. God made that promise to Adam and Eve (and to the entire world) after the fall into sin. God promised that he would send a Savior into the world to save the world. That promise is found in Genesis chapter 3, but God also promised, in Isaiah chapter 40, that he would send a prophet to prepare the way for this Savior to come.

That prophet was John the Baptist. John the Baptist needed to prepare the way for the Lord because by nature the people of the world could not see the light; they wouldn't understand their need for a Savior nor would Jesus be the Savior they would want. So John prepared the way with a message of repentance.

People who see their sin also see their need for a Savior. People who are told that a light, the Savior, is coming into the world start looking and waiting for that light to come. To those whose hearts had been prepared with a message of repentance, John could point to Jesus and say with a smile on his face, "Look! The Lamb of God, who takes away the sin of the world!" (John 1:29).

John the Baptist was a witness who testified concerning the light. Isn't that what we are? Aren't we witnesses too? Aren't we people whom God has called to continue to prepare the way of the Lord in a world that still, by nature, can't see the light, in a world that doesn't see a need for a Savior? As people who have seen the light, we can shine that light on others.

*Lord Jesus, make me a faithful witness of both you and your Word. Help me share both the law and the gospel in my own corner of the world. Bless my witnessing and enable me to know what to say and when to say it. Amen.*

# Well Received?

## John 1:10-13

*He was in the world, and the world was made through him, yet the world did not recognize him. He came to what was his own, yet his own people did not accept him. But to all who did receive him, to those who believe in his name, he gave the right to become children of God. They were born, not of blood, or of the desire of the flesh, or of a husband's will, but born of God.*

Amazing. Absolutely amazing. It's amazing that the one who created the world (the Creator) was not recognized by the world (the creation) when he came into the world. It's absolutely amazing that God's Old Testament people, for the most part, did not receive the Messiah for whom they had been eagerly waiting when he finally came into the world. Yet those two truths emphasize just how much sin darkens the heart of human beings. By nature, none of us would recognize the Son of God, the Creator of the world, the Savior of all—we were spiritually blind. By nature, none of us wanted to receive Jesus of Nazareth as the promised Messiah—we were spiritual enemies of God.

Amazing. Absolutely amazing. It's amazing that in spite of our spiritual blindness, in spite of being God's spiritual enemies, in spite of our stubbornness, and in spite of our refusal to see or want Jesus as our Savior, God gave us the right to become his children. Amazing. God's grace and mercy are always fascinating. Our faith, our ability to believe, and our adoption into God's family had nothing to do with us; it had everything to do with God. Our spiritual birth was not natural. It was not based on human decisions (our own decision for Christ). It was not the result of our parents' or our spouse's will. It was the will of

God that you and I believe in Jesus. It is the will of God that you and I are his redeemed children and heirs of eternal life.

Amazing.

*Holy Spirit, may I never take your gift of faith for granted. Forgive me for my human pride that wants to take some credit for being brought into God's family. Every day, help me marvel at God's amazing grace he has shown me in Christ. Amen.*

---

## Made Flesh

### John 1:14

*The Word became flesh and dwelled among us. We have seen his glory, the glory he has as the only-begotten from the Father, full of grace and truth.*

Think for a moment about the first four words of this verse. "The Word became flesh." Wow!

The eternal God, the second person of the Trinity, the one who was active in the creation of the world—he, God, became flesh, human flesh. God humbled himself by becoming one of us—one of us! A human being! He made his dwelling among us—he lived among human beings. Literally, John says that Jesus "tented" among us. Jesus is Immanuel—"God with us"—because in the person of Jesus Christ, the Word came to live among us.

Yet God didn't become flesh just so that he could live among us; he came so that he could live for us. God became flesh so that he could be our substitute—our substitute in life who would live a perfect life of obedience to God in our place and our substitute in death who would pay the wages of our sin.

It is in this substitute that we see God's glory. God's glory is revealed to us in his loving and gracious plan of salvation that was perfectly carried out in time by the God-man, the "Word-flesh," Jesus Christ.

The Word became flesh. Wow!

*Lord Jesus Christ, I thank you for your amazing love for me—a love that moved you to make yourself nothing, to take on the very nature of a servant, so that you could become obedient to death, even death on a cross—a death, the death, that paid for my sin. Amen.*

# A Riddle?

**John 1:15-18**

*John testified about him. He cried out, "This was the one I spoke about when I said, 'The one coming after me outranks me because he existed before me.' " For out of his fullness we have all received grace upon grace. For the law was given through Moses; grace and truth came through Jesus Christ. No one has ever seen God. The only-begotten Son, who is close to the Father's side, has made him known.*

"What?" That might be our response to these four verses if we were to read them through too quickly. John doesn't seem to make any sense. He seems to be speaking in riddles: "The one coming after me outranks me because he existed before me." The riddle is solved when we realize that it comes from John the Baptist talking about the eternal nature of Jesus—the Word made flesh. John the Baptist came on the scene first, baptizing by the Jordan River. Jesus showed up after John had already been preaching his message of repentance. But John the Baptist knew that this man was more than a man, he was the eternal Son of God in human flesh.

This God-man is the bringer—he is the giver—of God's grace. In fact, this God-man will always have more grace than we could ever possibly need or use. We never have to fear that we will use up God's grace.

God has more grace than we have sin.

God has more grace than we have sorrow.

God has more grace than we have worry.

God has more grace than we have sadness.

God has more grace than we have fear.

"For out of his fullness we have all received grace upon grace." Literally John wrote that Jesus will give us grace in place of grace. Like the candy bars in a vending machine, when one candy bar drops down from its shelf to the bottom of the machine for someone to take, another one immediately fills its place. But with God's grace we never have to be concerned that we will ever show up at God's vending machine of grace and see an empty row of candy bars. God has more grace than we have needs—God shows us his grace in every time of need.

*Heavenly Father, thank you for letting me see your grace, for letting me see you, in the face of your Son, my Savior, Jesus. Amen.*

# Who Are You?

## John 1:19-23

*This is the testimony John gave when the Jews from Jerusalem sent priests and Levites to ask him, "Who are you?"*

*He confessed and did not deny. He confessed, "I am not the Christ."*

*And they asked him, "Who are you then? Are you Elijah?"*

*He said, "I am not."*

*"Are you the Prophet?"*

*"No," he answered.*

*Then they asked him, "Who are you? Tell us so we can give an answer to those who sent us. What do you say about yourself?"*

*He said, "I am the voice of one crying out in the wilderness, 'Make straight the way of the Lord,' just as Isaiah the prophet said."*

John the Baptist and his message of repentance were causing quite a stir, so much so that the religious leaders back in Jerusalem felt compelled to check up on him out by the waters of the Jordan River.

Keep in mind that the people were waiting. The people of John's day were waiting for the Messiah to come, but they were also waiting for the second Elijah (perhaps Elijah himself brought back) and the prophet from among their own brothers whom Moses had said God would raise up.

Was John the Christ—the promised Messiah? Was he Elijah? Was he the prophet? The religious leaders needed to know who was causing this stir in the wilderness. They needed to know what his agenda was and why people were rushing out to see him.

John told them who he was. He told them exactly who he was. He was not the Christ. He was not Elijah (though Jesus would later tell his disciples that John the Baptist was the Elijah who was to come). He was not the prophet. Who was he? He was the promised forerunner of the Christ, the one whom Isaiah said would prepare the way of the Lord. The way of the Lord is prepared one way and one way alone—through a message of repentance.

*Holy Spirit, lead me to see my sin. Help me understand just how much my sin offends the holy God. Use your Holy Word to lead me to repentance—to see my sin, acknowledge it, confess it, ask God for forgiveness, trust that he forgives me for the sake of Christ, avoid those sins in the future, and correct with God's help whatever wrongs I can. Amen.*

---

## Someone Worth Talking About

### John 1:24-28

*They had been sent from the Pharisees. So they asked John, "Why then do you baptize, if you are not the Christ, or Elijah, or the Prophet?"*

*"I baptize with water," John answered. "Among you stands one you do not know. He is the one coming after me, whose sandal strap I am not worthy to untie."*

*These things happened in Bethany beyond the Jordan, where John was baptizing.*

The priests and Levites hadn't really gotten anywhere with John when they questioned him, so some Pharisees who had been sent from Jerusalem took over the interrogation. They wanted to know by whose authority John was doing all this baptizing—a valid question since as the religious leaders of the day, they were responsible for the spiritual well-being of the people.

Notice John's response. He could have talked about himself and his call from God, but instead he turned all the focus and attention on Jesus, a man whom John did not even feel worthy enough to serve as a slave. John wanted these Pharisees to know the one to come after him. John wanted the Pharisees to know the one that they did not know. John wanted the Pharisees to know the one who stood among them. John wanted the Pharisees to know Jesus, the Lamb of God who takes away the sin of the world.

Isn't that our goal too? Isn't it our goal to be humble enough to take the focus off ourselves when people want to compliment us or build us up and instead put the focus on Jesus? Isn't it our goal to direct others away from us and to the one whom they may not yet know? Isn't it our goal to point to Jesus and his cross and say to our friends, relatives, neighbors, and total strangers, "Look! The Lamb of God, who takes away the sin of the world!"? Of course it is!

*Holy Spirit, make me a humble and faithful witness of the one who came to save not only me but the entire world from sin. Amen.*

## The Lamb of God

### John 1:29-31

*The next day, John saw Jesus coming toward him and said, "Look! The Lamb of God, who takes away the sin of the world! This is the one I was talking about when I said, 'The one coming after me outranks me because he existed before me.' I myself did not know who he was, but I came baptizing with water so that he would be revealed to Israel."*

For countless years, God's people had been observing the Passover and sacrificing countless one-year-old male lambs without blemish or defect. For countless years, God's people had been offering the daily sacrifices required by him for their sin and guilt. These animals, these sacrifices, these offerings, the blood that was shed from generation after generation all pointed to the Passover Lamb whom God had promised to send.

Now picture yourself standing among the crowds by the Jordan River when suddenly John the Baptist says, "Look!" His command grabs your attention. You turn your head. You focus your attention, but all you see is a man, a fellow Jew just like you. Then you hear the improbable: "The Lamb of God, who takes away the sin of the world!" This is the promised Lamb? This is the Passover Lamb? Jesus of Nazareth?

"This is the one I've been telling you about! This is the one I told you would come! This is the one who is greater than I! This is the one who will shed his blood and die for your sins—and the sins of the whole world!"

What does this mean for us? We don't offer sacrifices to God, do we? We don't offer sin offerings and guilt offerings, do we? We don't observe the Passover, do we? Why? Because Jesus paid for sin once and for all with his death on the cross. There is no longer any need for any other sacrifices for sin. Our sin is paid for! Our guilt before God has been removed by the Lamb of God who takes away the sin of the world!

*Thank you, Jesus, for sacrificing your perfect life on the cross as payment for my sin. In view of your mercy, empower me to offer my life to you as a living sacrifice, one that is holy and pleasing to you. Amen.*

## Need a Sign?

**John 1:32-34**

> *John also testified, "I saw the Spirit descend like a dove from heaven and remain on him. I myself did not recognize him, but the one who sent me to baptize with water said to me, 'The one on whom you see the Spirit descend and remain, he is the one who will baptize with the Holy Spirit.' I saw this myself and have testified that this is the Son of God."*

Many times, people look for signs. Many times, people ask God for signs. "Lord, tell me what I should do. Should I take this job? Should I move to this town or that? Give me a sign so that I know what I'm supposed to do." Then they start looking for signs in the weather, the stars, a license plate from an out-of-state car.

God doesn't promise us such signs. God doesn't even tell us to ask for such signs. God, rather, encourages us to live by faith, not by sight. He calls us to trust him. He calls us to step out in faith. He calls us to put the common sense—the Christian common sense—that he has given us to good use. To ask and look for signs that he has not promised is, in reality, not trusting God and not living by faith.

John didn't ask God for a sign, but God gave him a sign. God gave him a sign not about where to live or what job to take; he gave him a sign regarding the one who would come after him. God promised that he would point out to him exactly who the promised Savior would be—the one whose way he was preparing. "The one on whom you see the Spirit descend and remain, he is the one." At Jesus' baptism, John saw the Holy Spirit come down on Jesus in the form of a dove and remain on him. John had no doubt about who Jesus was or who the promised Messiah was—they were one and the same. God had given him a sign. That sign was for our benefit. John tells us, "I saw it all. You can believe me that Jesus is the Savior whom God has sent."

*Help me, Holy Spirit, to live my life by faith. Assure me every day that, though I do not see Jesus with my physical eyes, my eyes of faith see him as my Savior from sin. While I asked for no sign of my salvation, I thank you for the empty tomb of Jesus that assures me that my sin is paid for. Amen.*

---

## Are You Following Me?
### John 1:35-42

*The next day, John was standing there again with two of his disciples. When John saw Jesus passing by, he said, "Look! The Lamb of God!" The two disciples heard him say this, and they followed Jesus.*

*When Jesus turned around and saw them following him, he asked, "What are you looking for?"*

*They said to him, "Rabbi" (which means "Teacher"),*
*"where are you staying?"*

*He told them, "Come, and you will see." So they came*
*and saw where he was staying. They stayed with him that*
*day. It was about the tenth hour.*

*Andrew, Simon Peter's brother, was one of the two who*
*heard John and followed Jesus. The first thing Andrew*
*did was to find his own brother Simon and say to him,*
*"We have found the Messiah!" (which is translated "the*
*Christ"). He brought him to Jesus.*

*Looking at him, Jesus said, "You are Simon, son of*
*Jonah. You will be called Cephas" (which means "Peter").*

Are you following me? This is the question implied when John the Baptist once again pointed two of his disciples to Jesus, the Lamb of God. In pointing Andrew, and most likely John, to Jesus, John the Baptist was saying, "The time has come for you to stop following me and start following Jesus."

Are you following me? This is the question Jesus implied as he turned around and asked these two former disciples of John the Baptist, "What are you looking for?" They wanted to follow Jesus. They wanted to spend time with the Lamb of God. They wanted to be disciples—followers and students—of the promised Messiah.

Are you following me? This is the question we can picture Andrew asking his brother Peter after he told him they had found the Messiah. Andrew told his brother Peter, "I'm following him. I'm staying with him. I am one of his disciples. I came here to get you. Are you following me back to Jesus?"

Are you following me? That is a question Jesus could ask each one of us every day. That is a question that convicts guilty consciences because we know that many times our actions, our words, and our thoughts are not in step with someone who is supposed to be following Jesus.

Are you following me? is a question that becomes a call to repentance.

Are you following me? ultimately becomes a source of great comfort for us who do repent. In asking us that question, Jesus reminds us just who it is we are following. We are following the Lamb of God. And what did that Lamb of God do? He took away the sin of the world. He took away my sin!

*Lord Jesus, thank you for calling me to be your disciple, for giving me the privilege of following you. Knowing that in you alone I have eternal life, equip, empower, and motivate me to follow you each day in all I do, say, and think. Amen.*

---

## Come and See

### John 1:43-51

*The next day, Jesus wanted to leave for Galilee. He found Philip and said to him, "Follow me." Now Philip was from Bethsaida, the hometown of Andrew and Peter.*

*Philip found Nathanael and told him, "We have found the one Moses wrote about in the Law, and about whom the prophets also wrote—Jesus of Nazareth, the son of Joseph."*

*Nathanael said to him, "Nazareth! Can anything good come from there?"*

*"Come and see!" Philip told him.*

*Jesus saw Nathanael coming toward him and said about him, "Truly, here is an Israelite in whom there is no deceit."*

*Nathanael asked him, "How do you know me?"*

*Jesus answered, "Before Philip called you, while you were under the fig tree, I saw you."*

*Nathanael answered him, "Rabbi, you are the Son of God! You are the King of Israel!"*

*Jesus replied, "You believe because I told you that I saw you under the fig tree. You will see greater things than that!" Then he added, "Amen, Amen, I tell you: You will see heaven opened and the angels of God ascending and descending on the Son of Man."*

In the previous verses, it was Andrew who just had to tell someone about Jesus. He went immediately, John said, and found his brother Peter. In these verses, it was Philip who just had to tell someone about Jesus. Philip found Nathanael and told him that Jesus of Nazareth was the promised Messiah, the one about whom all the Old Testament had been written.

Nathanael was skeptical—perhaps only for the simple reason that he knew the Savior was to come from Bethlehem and not from Nazareth. But Philip didn't get discouraged when Nathanael tried to dump this cold water of skepticism on his burning fire of faith, nor did he try to argue the point. He didn't try to convince Nathanael of anything; he simply invited him to "come and see!"

God took care of the rest. Jesus revealed himself to Nathanael as God's Son and the promised Messiah. The Holy Spirit turned Nathanael's Old Testament faith in the coming Messiah into New Testament faith in Jesus as the Messiah who had come.

Andrew told Peter. Philip told Nathanael. Both of them just had to tell someone about Jesus. What about you? Is there someone in your life with whom you can share Jesus? Will that be today? Tomorrow? Whenever God presents an opportunity to share Jesus with another person, let's take advantage of it and do so confidently, knowing that the Holy Spirit will work through our witnessing.

*Lord Jesus Christ, grant me the courageous desire to share my faith with others. Bless my witnessing that your kingdom may come to many others. Amen.*

---

# Water Into Wine

### John 2:1-11

*Three days later, there was a wedding in Cana of Galilee. Jesus' mother was there. Jesus and his disciples were also invited to the wedding.*

*When the wine was gone, Jesus' mother said to him, "They have no wine."*

*Jesus said to her, "Woman, what does that have to do with you and me? My time has not come yet."*

*His mother said to the servants, "Do whatever he tells you."*

*Six stone water jars, which the Jews used for ceremonial cleansing, were standing there, each holding twenty or thirty gallons. Jesus told them, "Fill the jars with water." So they filled them to the brim. Then he said to them, "Now draw some out and take it to the master of the banquet." And they did.*

*When the master of the banquet tasted the water that had now become wine, he did not know where it came from (though the servants who had drawn the water knew). The master of the banquet called the bridegroom and said to him, "Everyone serves the good wine first, and when the guests have had plenty to drink, then the cheaper wine. You saved the good wine until now!"*

*This, the beginning of his miraculous signs, Jesus*

*performed in Cana of Galilee. He revealed his glory, and his disciples believed in him.*

The account of the wedding at Cana and Jesus turning water into wine may be a familiar one. It is easy, however, to get caught up in the details and the speculation surrounding this wedding reception. It is easy for some to draw conclusions and establish principles regarding the use of alcohol or the sanctity of marriage based on this account. This account has been used and misused as people debate Jesus' involvement in this time of need: Is Jesus promoting the use of alcohol? Is he condoning drunkenness? What does his presence at such an event signify? To some, Jesus becomes a target—look at how disrespectful he was of his mother. To some, he becomes an example of generous giving—look at how much wine, and the quality of that wine, he gave to this couple as a wedding gift, a gift that spared them embarrassment and humiliation.

Talking points for sure. Applications to be made—certainly. Opportunity to read one section of Scripture in the light of the rest of Scripture (as they pertain to marriage, drinking alcohol, the Fourth Commandment, and the fact that Jesus never sinned)—absolutely. But may we not miss the point of this miracle. Verse 11: "This, the beginning of his miraculous signs, Jesus performed in Cana of Galilee. He revealed his glory, and his disciples believed in him." This miracle gives us a glimpse of Jesus' divinity. This miracle reminds us that Jesus is more than just a man—he is the very Son of God who came to save us from our sin. May we too put our faith in him!

*Lord Jesus, I thank you for revealing your glory to me in your Word, specifically here in your first recorded miracle. May I never doubt that you are God my Savior. Amen.*

## Righteous Anger

**John 2:12-16**

*After this, he went down to Capernaum with his mother, brothers, and disciples, and they stayed there for a few days.*

*The Jewish Passover was near, so Jesus went up to Jerusalem.*

*In the temple courts he found people selling cattle, sheep, and doves, and money changers sitting at tables. He made a whip of cords and drove everyone out of the temple courts, along with the sheep and oxen. He scattered the coins of the money changers and overturned their tables. To those selling doves he said, "Get these things out of here! Stop turning my Father's house into a place of business!"*

The Lamb of God—the Passover Lamb—went up to Jerusalem to celebrate and observe the Jewish Passover. The Passover was an annual celebration and observance during which God's people were to remember and thank God for delivering them from slavery in Egypt (when God had them wipe the blood of those one-year-old male lambs around their door frames). It was also an annual celebration and observance during which God's people were to anticipate their deliverance from the slavery of sin through the shedding of the Passover Lamb's blood.

That's hardly what Jesus saw when he arrived at the temple in Jerusalem. God's people were not remembering, they were not thanking, they were not observing, they were not anticipating, they were not celebrating. God's house had been turned into a market filled with noisy, smelly animals; dishonest, greedy merchants; and worshipers more concerned about the outward rite and the letter of the law than true worship and sacrifice. Jesus was angry—and rightly so. His anger here—and again at the end of his ministry—has often been called a righteous anger. In righteous anger he pointed out sin and cleaned up God's house. In righteous anger he restored order and provided a place for meaningful worship.

An account like this reminds us of the purpose of gathering together for public worship. An account like this reminds us that we can come early to worship in order to prepare for it by considering the worship theme, the readings for the day, and the hymns. An account like this reminds us to be respectful of the other worshipers present by refraining from loud talk that can distract them prior to the service. An account like this reminds us of the privilege we have each week to gather around Word and sacrament. An account like this reminds us that the Lamb of God has come and he has taken away the sins of the world—he has taken away our sins! An account like this reminds us of the joy we experience when we bring our thank offerings to God.

*Help me always, Lord, to worship you in spirit and in truth. Amen.*

## Missing the Point

**John 2:17,18**

*His disciples remembered that it was written, "Zeal for your house will consume me."*
*So the Jews responded, "What sign are you going to show us to prove you can do these things?"*

Jesus' disciples did not miss the point of what their teacher had just done. Jesus had just driven the money changers and animals out of the temple area. In righteous anger he declared, "How dare you turn my Father's house into a market!" In Jesus' words and actions, the disciples saw the fulfillment of Scripture. The words of Psalm 69:9—a psalm containing prophecies about the coming Messiah—came to mind: "Zeal for your house will consume me." Like Jesus' miracle in Cana, this was another sign that pointed the disciples to Jesus as the promised Messiah.

The Jewish leaders, however, missed the point. After listening to Jesus' rebuke and seeing the way he drove those money changers and animals from the temple area, the Jewish leaders didn't thank Jesus. They didn't say, "It's about time someone restored order here." They didn't say, "God, we're sorry for the way we have been acting and for the careless way we have been leading your people and for the thoughtless way we have been treating your temple and all these sacrifices." No, rather than commending Jesus and his actions, they questioned him and his actions. They asked Jesus for a sign to prove that he had the authority to do what he had just done.

Ironic, really. Zeal for God's house was the sign! The disciples got it; the Jewish leaders did not. In the verses that follow, Jesus will give them another sign—there again, unfortunately, they will miss the point. May we never miss the point! Jesus is the one to whom all Scripture points. The Old Testament is full of passages that say, "The Savior is coming; watch for this sign." The New Testament is full of passages that say, "The Savior came; Jesus fulfilled every sign." There's the point—the point of Scripture. God kept his promise. He sent his Son to be our Savior.

*Holy Spirit, open my heart and increase my knowledge of your Word every time I read it, every time I hear it, and every time I study it. Help me to read all of Scripture in the light of Jesus and what he has done for me to save me from my sin. Amen.*

# The Sign

## John 2:19-22

> *Jesus answered them, "Destroy this temple, and in three days I will raise it up again."*
>
> *The Jews said, "It took forty-six years to build this temple! And you are going to raise it in three days?" But Jesus was speaking about the temple of his body. When Jesus was raised from the dead, his disciples remembered that he had said this. Then they believed the Scripture and what Jesus had said.*

The Jewish leaders had missed the point of what Jesus had just done. When Jesus cleared the temple of the money changers and animals, they failed to see their sin, they failed to confess it, they failed to repent. We ended the previous devotion, however, with the Jewish leaders asking Jesus for a sign to prove that he had authority to do what he had just done. We can actually commend them for this. They were the religious leaders of the day; they were the ones charged by God to be responsible for the temple and the worship life of the people. While they had failed to keep the focus of worship and those sacrifices and the Passover on the Lamb who was to come, they did understand that they needed to ask someone who had just come into the temple area and done what Jesus had done what right he had to do that.

Once again they missed the point, though. Jesus gave them a sign. He said, "Destroy this temple, and in three days I will raise it up again." They assumed he was talking about the temple building near which they were standing. Notice, though, that Jesus didn't say he would destroy the temple—as they would accuse him of in three short years—he told them that when they destroyed this temple, he would raise it in three days.

John gives us the insight that even he and the other disciples didn't have at the time but that they came to realize after Jesus' resurrection—the temple Jesus was talking about was his body. These same Jewish leaders would destroy that temple when they demanded Pilate to crucify him. The destruction of the temple of Jesus' body paid for the sins of the world. Jesus raised the temple of his body three days later—just as promised—when he rose from the dead, the sign that he not only had authority to cleanse the temple that day but that he had indeed paid for the sins of the world and that he truly is the Son of God.

*I could never thank you enough, Jesus, for your death and resurrection, but may my life reflect my gratitude for your free forgiveness. Amen.*

---

## Expectations

**John 2:23-25**

> *While he was in Jerusalem for the Passover Festival, many believed in his name as they observed the miraculous signs he was doing. But Jesus, on his part, was not entrusting himself to them, because he knew them all. He did not need anyone to testify about man, because he himself knew what was in man.*

The people in Jerusalem had heard of and seen the miracles Jesus had been performing. Suddenly, they all had expectations of him. "Jesus can make me—or my loved one—healthy. Jesus can make my life better. Jesus can make my life easy. I can ride his coattails to fame and popularity and power." So while Jesus was popular, he didn't let that popularity go to his head, nor did he get caught up in the excitement of having all those followers. Rather, as one who can see and know the heart of each human being, Jesus understood that many of those people were following him for the wrong reasons; he knew that many of those people would eventually stop following him.

Expectations. What do we expect from Jesus? If we were to analyze the prayers that we addressed to him this past week, what would we find? Did our prayers tend to focus on what Jesus could do for us in this life—restore health, bless a surgery, heal a relationship, take away some pain, help with an interview, improve our family finances, provide what we need in life? To be sure, we have the right as God's children to bring those requests to Jesus and expect—even trust—that Jesus can and will help. But is that all we expect of Jesus? To make life here on earth better for us?

May the Holy Spirit enable us to balance our requests, prayers, and petitions. May we remember that the primary reason Jesus came was to save us from our sin. May we take those problems— our sins—to Jesus, to confess them and ask for his forgiveness and the faith to believe that we are forgiven. May our prayers be filled with thanksgiving. How can they not be? We're going to heaven one day! Because of Jesus, we have every right to expect that!

*Lord Jesus, help me to see you first as my Savior from sin; help me to seek first your righteousness and know that all the other things of life can be added to me as well. Amen.*

## Born Again

### John 3:1-6

*There was a man of the Pharisees named Nicodemus, a member of the Jewish ruling council. He came to Jesus at night and said to him, "Rabbi, we know that you are a teacher who has come from God, for no one can do these miraculous signs you are doing unless God is with him."*

*Jesus replied, "Amen, Amen, I tell you: Unless someone is born from above, he cannot see the kingdom of God."*

*Nicodemus said to him, "How can a man be born when he is old? He cannot enter a second time into his mother's womb and be born, can he?"*

*Jesus answered, "Amen, Amen, I tell you: Unless someone is born of water and the Spirit, he cannot enter the kingdom of God! Whatever is born of the flesh is flesh. Whatever is born of the Spirit is spirit."*

Typically, whenever the Pharisees came to ask Jesus questions, it was to try to trap him, embarrass him, or discredit him. That's not the case in John chapter 3 with Nicodemus. Nicodemus, a Pharisee as well as a member of the Sanhedrin, knew the Old Testament. He had read it. He had been taught it. He had even taught it to others. Then he heard Jesus teach it. He heard Jesus—the one who had also been performing miracles—teach about the kingdom of God, and he knew that Jesus was no ordinary teacher. He wanted to know more. He wanted to learn more. He went to the Teacher.

The first thing Jesus taught Nicodemus was something called the doctrine of original sin. He taught Nicodemus that all human beings are born in sin; we are all born spiritually dead and spiritually blind; we all come into this world as spiritual enemies of God who want nothing to do with him. We have nothing good in us—no redeeming qualities. Jesus said, "No one can see the kingdom of God unless he is born again."

Nicodemus granted the fact that he knew Jesus was not talking about a second physical birth, but he also conceded that he was not exactly sure what Jesus meant by a second birth. Jesus explained that in order to enter the kingdom of God, we need to be born of water and the Spirit—we need to be baptized. When we were baptized—when we were born again—the Holy Spirit made us spiritually alive, adopted us into God's family, washed away our sins, robed us in the righteousness of Jesus, made us heirs of eternal life, and now empowers us to daily drown our old Adam in contrition and repentance.

So, are you a born-again Christian? There really is no other kind of Christian!

*Thank you, Holy Spirit, for working through the water and the Word in Baptism to make me spiritually alive so that I can enter God's eternal kingdom. Amen.*

## How Can This Be?

**John 3:7-13**

*"Do not be surprised when I tell you that you must be born from above. The wind blows where it pleases. You hear its sound, but you do not know where it comes from or where it is going. So it is with everyone who is born of the Spirit."*

*"How can these things be?" asked Nicodemus.*

*"You are the teacher of Israel," Jesus answered, "and you do not know these things? Amen, Amen, I tell you:*

*We speak what we know, and we testify about what we*
*have seen. But you people do not accept our testimony.*
*If I have told you earthly things and you do not believe,*
*how will you believe if I tell you heavenly things? No one*
*has ascended into heaven, except the one who descended*
*from heaven, the Son of Man, who is in heaven."*

Jesus had just finished telling Nicodemus that in order for people to enter the kingdom of God, they must be born again. Nicodemus replied by asking, "How can this be?" He asked the same question here in response to Jesus. "How can this be?" Nicodemus was wondering out loud when and where God would send the Holy Spirit into the hearts of people to make them spiritually alive.

Jesus used the illustration of the wind. We don't know where the wind comes from or when it will blow, but we know it is blowing when it finally does come. We don't know where the Spirit comes from or when he will come, but we know he is in our hearts when he finally does come.

Jesus was disappointed that one of Israel's teachers did not understand the earthly side of conversion, the things that happen here on earth: rebirth, God's gift of faith, repentance, Baptism. Jesus' point was that if we don't understand the earthly side of conversion—repentance, faith, rebirth, Baptism—how will we ever understand the heavenly side of conversion: where and when the Holy Spirit will work. Jesus did assure Nicodemus, however, that while human beings may not understand these things, the Son of Man—the one who came from heaven— certainly does.

Lest we join Nicodemus in his confusion, the point for us is that while we may not know when or where the Holy Spirit will come with his gift of faith (or upon whom he will come), we do know the means through which he will come and we have those means at our disposal—the means of grace. We have God's promise that the Holy Spirit will bring his gifts of rebirth, repentance, and faith through the gospel in both Word and sacrament.

*Come, Holy Spirit, and kindle in my heart the fire of your love. Amen.*

## Look Up and Live

### John 3:14,15

*"Just as Moses lifted up the snake in the wilderness, so the Son of Man must be lifted up, so that everyone who believes in him shall not perish but have eternal life."*

In the Old Testament, the people of Israel often grumbled and complained as they wandered for 40 years in the wilderness. On one occasion, as the people spoke out against God—saying that it would have been better to remain slaves in Egypt than to die in the desert—God sent venomous snakes among the people. Many of the Israelites died from those snakebites. The people, however, repented. Moses intervened. God answered their prayer—he did not take the venomous snakes away, but he did provide help. He told Moses to make a snake out of bronze and put it on a pole. Then God attached this promise to the bronze snake: Anyone who was bitten by one of those venomous snakes could look up in faith at the bronze snake and live. (To be sure, this bronze snake was not an idol. The Israelites were not looking to the bronze snake for healing. Rather, in Spirit-worked faith and trust of God's promise of healing, they looked up and lived.)

Speaking to Nicodemus (a man who knew his Old Testament and would have been very familiar with the account of the bronze snake in Numbers chapter 21) in John chapter 3, Jesus said, "Just as Moses lifted up the snake in the wilderness, so the Son of Man must be lifted up, so that everyone who believes in him shall not perish but have eternal life."

Jesus was "lifted up" when the Roman soldiers nailed him to a cross and jammed that cross into the ground. On the cross—lifted up—Jesus suffered and died to pay for our sins. God attached a promise to Jesus' suffering and death—the same promise he had attached to the bronze snake: "Look up and live." We who have been bitten by the snakebite of sin—a bite that could kill us eternally—can look up in faith to Jesus, trusting God's promise that everyone who believes in him will have eternal life.

*Holy Spirit, I thank you for lifting my eyes of faith to Jesus. I thank you for your gift of faith that trusts God's promises and receives his blessings of forgiveness and life. Amen.*

---

## Love in Action

### John 3:16

*"For God so loved the world that he gave his only-begotten Son, that whoever believes in him shall not perish, but have eternal life."*

The most well-known verse in Scripture? Perhaps.
The most important verse of Scripture? Maybe.
But does it ever become cliché? Do we ever just rattle it off from memory and not consider the depth of its meaning and

significance? Do we ever just read right over it as if to say, "I've heard this all before; I know all this; tell me something more"?

What more could there possibly be?

God loved the world. Think about that! God loved the world—the sinful, rebellious, selfish, arrogant, stubborn, complaining, and discontent world. God loved the unlovable. God loved me! Yet God's love isn't just an emotion, attitude, or feeling; it's an action. God's love for the sinful world—God's love for me—moved him to act, to act on my behalf. God's love moved him to have compassion on me and show me mercy by sending his Son into the world as the one and only sacrifice that would satisfy his justice, the one and only sacrifice that would spare me from the fires of hell. And Jesus—in love—actually was willing to come and be that sacrifice! Love in action.

The promise that God—in love—attaches to that sacrifice is the promise we heard in reference to the bronze snake: look up and live! Whoever believes in him—in Jesus—shall not perish but will have eternal life. Love in action, right? Not only did God—in love—spare us from the punishment we deserved, but he also—in love—gave us life in heaven, which we did not deserve. Love in action!

And all this because God the Holy Spirit—in love—gave us his gift of faith in Jesus!

*Thank you, God, for so loving me. Thank you for sending your one and only Son so that by your gracious gift of faith, I who believe in him will not perish but have eternal life. Amen.*

# No Condemnation

### John 3:17,18

*"For God did not send his Son into the world to condemn the world, but to save the world through him. The one who believes in him is not condemned, but the one who does not believe is condemned already, because he has not believed in the name of the only-begotten Son of God."*

Still speaking to Nicodemus, Jesus emphasized what he had just said in verse 16: God the Father sent his Son into the world for one reason and one reason alone: to save the world. We say it again, "God sent his Son into the world to save the world."

Which word should we focus on in that simple sentence? *God? His Son? Sent? Into? Save?* We could focus on any or all of them. We could mention the grace, mercy, and compassion that God the Father had for sinners. We could mention the willingness, love, and determination of his Son to be our Savior. We could mention the divine intervention required and given in the simple word *sent.* We could talk about Jesus' incarnation and his state of humiliation—the fact that he became nothing, that he was obedient to death—as we focus on that simple word *into.* We could talk about the blessed results as we delve into the various aspects of being saved—what he saved us from (the hell we deserved) and what he saved us for (the heaven we don't deserve). All would be a fitting application and meaningful discussion.

But what about the word *world*? Jesus came to save the world. Perhaps Nicodemus and the other Jews felt that the Messiah would only save them, God's chosen people. Perhaps the Gentiles felt that there was no hope for them since they were not part of God's chosen people. No, Jesus says. He came to save the world. He came to save all. He came to save all and condemn none.

What Jesus did as the God-man in both his life and death he did for all—he did it for you, he did it for me, and he did it for the world. Forgiveness, life, and salvation are there for all who believe. Forgiveness, life, and salvation are there for you. In Christ, there is no condemnation.

*Holy Spirit, strengthen my faith in Jesus that I may never forfeit the salvation I have in him. Amen.*

---

# Exposed

### John 3:19-21

*"This is the basis for the judgment: The light has come into the world, yet people loved the darkness rather than the light, because their deeds were evil. In fact, everyone who practices wicked things hates the light and does not come toward the light, or else his deeds would be exposed. But the one who does what is true comes toward the light, in order that his deeds may be seen as having been done in connection with God."*

By nature, every person in this world loves evil. In fact, more attractive to the unbelieving heart and mind than Jesus and his light and love are the evil deeds of darkness. The heart of a sinful human being is drawn not to Christ but to the selfish sins of the flesh. Not only is the heart of a sinful human being not drawn to the light of Christ, but it actually strives to avoid that light at all costs because it does not want that light to expose its selfish immorality for what it truly is—sin that condemns.

None of that, however, stopped the light from coming into the world. But, as John already told us in his gospel, Jesus came into the world not to condemn the world but to save the world. The light of Christ changes the heart of sinful human beings. Exposing the deeds of darkness brings repentance. Repentance brings forgiveness. There is a change. A light goes on. Call it faith. The newborn child of God lives in the light. Christ's light shines in and through us. Our lives lived in the light bring glory to the one who brought us "out of darkness into his marvelous light" (1 Peter 2:9).

*Thank you, Jesus, for your light of truth—a light that exposed my sin but a light that also pointed a bright beacon of faith on you, my Savior. Help me to walk and live in the light. Amen.*

## Competition

### John 3:22-26

*After this, Jesus and his disciples went into the Judean countryside where he spent some time with them and was baptizing.*

*John also was baptizing in Aenon near Salim, because there was plenty of water there. People kept coming and were being baptized, for John had not been thrown into prison yet.*

*Then an argument broke out between John's disciples and a certain Jew about purification. His disciples came to John and said to him, "Rabbi, the one who was with you across the Jordan, about whom you testified—look, he is baptizing, and everyone is going to him!"*

This incident took place very early in Jesus' public ministry and near the end of John the Baptist's public ministry, before he was put in prison. Both Jesus and John were in the Judean countryside—in close but separate proximity. Both of them were baptizing and, no doubt, preaching that same message of repentance that each had been proclaiming prior to this. It soon became apparent to John's disciples that "everyone" was going to Jesus and none (fewer and fewer) were coming out to them. Jealousy. Competition. We'll hear what John the Baptist said in response to this in the verses that follow.

For now, we focus briefly on our own attitudes toward public ministry, called workers, our fellow congregations and schools, and different ministry groups within our own congregation. God is the one who blesses public servants and their ministries—be they pastors, teachers, staff ministers, or missionaries. God is the one who blesses the ministries of our congregations and schools and individual boards, committees, and groups. We are all on the same team. We all have the same goals and prayers and purpose. Competition and jealousy are out of place. Rather, may we thank God for all the blessings he gives to his church through his called servants and laypeople. May we rejoice with a fellow congregation, school, or congregational group when God blesses their ministry. Ministry work is not a competition; it is an answer to the Second Petition of the Lord's Prayer when we ask that God's kingdom would come to us and many others.

*Bless the efforts, Lord, of all who preach, teach, and share your Word. Amen.*

## Knowing My Role

### John 3:27-30

> John answered, "A man cannot receive a single thing,
> unless it has been given to him from heaven. You your-
> selves are witnesses that I said, 'I am not the Christ, but I
> have been sent ahead of him.' The one who has the bride
> is the bridegroom. But the friend of the bridegroom, who
> stands and listens for him, is overjoyed when he hears the
> bridegroom's voice. So this joy of mine is now complete.
> He must increase, but I must decrease."

John the Baptist's disciples were frustrated and jealous because everyone was going out to see, hear, and be baptized by Jesus and no one was coming out to them and their teacher. John used this opportunity to explain to his disciples that each of us has a role to play in God's kingdom and those roles and the abilities to carry out those roles are given to us by God himself.

John's God-given role was to prepare the way for Christ, to point people to Christ. The very goal of his ministry was to work himself out of a job. The time was supposed to come and had now come when people were to stop following him and start following Jesus. The time had come for Jesus and his ministry to become greater and more important and for John and his ministry to become less, but John found joy in that. He found joy in faithfully acknowledging and carrying out his role.

We each have roles in the church of God. The roles are all different, but God has given each of us the abilities and gifts to serve faithfully in those roles. More than that, those roles themselves have been given to us by God. Embrace your role, whatever that role may be—a mother, a lay leader in the church, a sister, a husband, a student, an usher, a Christian friend, a light shining in this dark world. The list could go on. Embrace your role—your roles!—and humbly serve; serve in such a way that all you do points not to self but to Christ.

*Take my life and let it be consecrated, Lord, to thee. Amen.*

---

## Greater Testimony

### John 3:31-36

> *The one who comes from above is superior to everyone. The one who is from the earth belongs to the earth and speaks in a way that belongs to the earth. The one who comes from heaven is superior to everyone. He testifies about what he has seen and heard, yet no one receives his testimony. The one who has received his testimony has certified that God is true. In fact, the one whom God has sent speaks God's words, for God gives the Spirit without measure. The Father loves the Son and has put everything in his hands. The one who believes in the Son has eternal life, but the one who rejects the Son will not see life; instead, God's wrath remains on him.*

John the Baptist had just pointed out to his disciples that Jesus and his ministry and following should be greater than his. John's ministry had served its purpose; he had prepared the way of the Lord.

But the apostle John now points out another reason why Jesus and his ministry were greater than John the Baptist's. Jesus came from heaven; John had come from the earth. Jesus is above all. He is the Son of God. God the Father had sent him to earth with the message of truth, the very words of God. He had placed everything into Jesus' hands. His testimony should have been (and always was) greater than John the Baptist's.

And yet, the apostle John says, "no one" accepted his testimony. There were indeed times of popularity in the life and ministry of Jesus, but most fell away on account of him. Many were not looking for a Messiah like him or the salvation he came to offer. In spite of that, God's promise remains, and God still gives his Spirit without limit—"The one who believes in the Son has eternal life." We have eternal life through the Spirit's gift of faith in the one whom God sent from heaven.

*Though I speak as one from the earth, Lord, though you did not send me from heaven, use me and my witness to send your Holy Spirit into the hearts of still more that they too may believe in your Son and have eternal life. Amen.*

## No Coincidence

### John 4:1-6

*Jesus found out that the Pharisees had heard he was making and baptizing more disciples than John, though it was not Jesus himself who was baptizing but his disciples. So he left Judea and went back again to Galilee.*

*He had to go through Samaria. So he came to a town in Samaria called Sychar, near the piece of land Jacob gave to his son Joseph. Jacob's well was there. Then Jesus, being tired from the journey, sat down by the well. It was about the sixth hour.*

The rising popularity of Jesus was a growing concern for the Pharisees. Resentment of Jesus and his ministry and following had already begun to spring up and take root in their hearts. This was not the time in Jesus' life, however, for their animosity to reach a boiling point. This was not the time in God's plan of salvation for Jesus to be put on trial and interrogated. Knowing all this, Jesus withdrew. Jesus headed north, back into Galilee, and allowed things to settle down in Judea.

Jesus could have taken any number of routes to head back to Galilee. He happened to choose the road less traveled by the Jews. That road went straight through Samaria. Jews avoided that route because they detested the Samaritans; Jews avoided that route because they didn't want any trouble. It's no coincidence that Jesus chose this route. There was a certain Samaritan woman whom he planned to meet. There was a certain Samaritan woman who needed to meet him.

Chapter 3 ended with the words "The one who believes in the Son has eternal life, but the one who rejects the Son will not see life." "The one who believes" applies to both Jews and Gentiles. Jesus came for all. Jesus died for all. Jesus reached out to all. That includes you and me. Jesus came for us. Jesus died for us. Jesus reached out to us and brought us to faith in him; he gave us life—spiritual and eternal life. As we consider Jesus' conversation with this woman at the well, may we be reminded that today Jesus reaches out to others through us. It's no coincidence that he uses us who know his Word to share his Word with those who don't.

*Help me, Lord, to see the people you place in front of me every day who need to hear your Word. Give me the courage to reach out to them with your Word of Truth. Amen.*

## Living Water

### John 4:7-15

*A woman from Samaria came to draw water. Jesus said to her, "Give me a drink." (His disciples had gone into town to buy food.)*

*The Samaritan woman said to him, "How is it that you, a Jew, ask for a drink from me, a Samaritan woman?" (For Jews do not associate with Samaritans.)*

*Jesus answered her, "If you knew the gift of God and who it is that is saying to you, 'Give me a drink,' you would have asked him, and he would have given you living water."*

*"Sir," she said, "you don't even have a bucket, and the well is deep. So where do you get this living water? You are not greater than our father Jacob, are you? He gave us this well and drank from it himself, as did his sons and his animals."*

*Jesus answered her, "Everyone who drinks this water will be thirsty again, but whoever drinks the water I will give him will never be thirsty ever again. Rather, the water I will give him will become in him a spring of water, bubbling up to eternal life."*

*"Sir, give me this water," the woman said to him, "so I won't get thirsty and have to keep coming here to draw water."*

John now tells us why Jesus had to go through Samaria—he had to meet this Samaritan woman. He had something to give her—living water that bubbles up to eternal life.

To this Samaritan woman's surprise, Jesus initiated the conversation. He asked her for a drink of water—a natural enough request except for the fact that it came from a Jewish man to a

Samaritan woman. Jesus could have lived without this drink of water (in fact, it seems he never did get it), but Jesus knew that this woman could not live eternally without drinking the water he had for her. Similar to his conversation with Nicodemus, Jesus bridged the the conversation from the physical to the spiritual. Similar to Nicodemus, the woman seemed to understand that Jesus wasn't necessarily talking about a literal drink of water, but she had to ask an obvious question to find out what exactly Jesus was talking about.

"If only you knew," Jesus was saying to himself. "If only you knew," Jesus was saying to her. "If only you knew whom you were talking to—yes, I'm greater than Jacob. My water is greater than his." Jesus has the life-giving, spiritual water of the Word. All who drink of this water will live forever. All who drink of this water will never thirst again. The woman still didn't understand—she began to think that if she had some of this magic water, her days of trekking out to the well to fetch water would be over. To help her understand this living water, Jesus will have to help her first see her spiritual thirst—which he will do in the verses that follow.

*So many times, Lord, I live and act as though I don't need the life-giving water of your Word. So many times, I ignorantly and arrogantly refuse to drink it—whether I decide to skip church or whether I fail to make time at home. Forgive me for despising your Word. Assure me of the forgiveness I have in Jesus. Help me to drink regularly and often from your life-giving Word. Amen.*

## Thirsty?

### John 4:16-18

*Jesus told her, "Go, call your husband, and come back here."*

*"I have no husband," the woman answered.*

*Jesus said to her, "You are right when you say, 'I have no husband.' In fact, you have had five husbands, and the man you have now is not your husband. What you have said is true."*

In order to drink and appreciate the life-giving water that Jesus wanted to share with this woman, she needed to first see and realize her spiritual thirst. Only the law—working as a mirror—could lead her to see her spiritual thirst. Jesus held up that mirror when he said, "Go, call your husband, and come back here." Jesus knew she had no husband. He knew that she had had five husbands, had been divorced several times, and was currently living with someone who was not her husband. Jesus knew all about her. He knew all about her adultery. He knew all about her sin. With his request that she go and get her husband, Jesus was opening the door for her to see her sin and confess it.

Admittedly, we don't know the tone with which she said, "I have no husband." We can't see into her heart. Perhaps she said this with her head down, full of shame, admitting her guilt. We pray that Jesus' use of the law served its intended purpose—to lead this woman to repentance and help her see her spiritual thirst and need for this living water.

Thirsty? One who runs 3 miles on a warm, sunny day is thirsty—a bottle of water or Gatorade is a no-brainer. One who practices football in the heat and humidity of August in full pads knows that drinking plenty of water is a necessity. Only when we see our sin and experience our guilt will the life-giving water of the Word be refreshing. So we use the law. We hold it up as a mirror to examine our own thoughts, words, and actions—our very lives—to see that every day we fall short of God's glory. May we all admit that. It is then, and only then, that Jesus can quench our thirst with his living water that bubbles up to eternal life.

*Lord, I confess my many sins. I have failed to do those things you command, and I have insisted on doing those things you forbid. Forgive me for the sake of Christ! Amen.*

---

# True Worship

### John 4:19-24

> *"Sir," the woman replied, "I see that you are a prophet. Our fathers worshipped on this mountain, but you Jews insist that the place where we must worship is in Jerusalem."*
>
> *Jesus said to her, "Believe me, woman, a time is coming when you will not worship the Father on this mountain or in Jerusalem. You Samaritans worship what you do not know. We worship what we do know, because salvation is from the Jews. But a time is coming and now is here when the real worshippers will worship the Father in spirit and in truth, for those are the kind of worshippers the Father seeks. God is spirit, and those who worship him must worship in spirit and in truth."*

In love, Jesus had just convicted this woman of her sins of adultery and divorce. Her comment that follows seems to be somewhat random. Perhaps she was trying to change the subject.

"Let's not talk about that—my adultery and divorce. Let's not talk about me." So she asked this out-of-the-blue question about worship—who can worship the Lord, where we should worship the Lord, etc. But maybe her question isn't all that random. Maybe she's not trying to change the subject. Maybe she's not ignoring Jesus' call to repentance. Maybe she's trying to figure out where to turn for forgiveness and how to turn there. "You got me, Jesus. You called a spade a spade. I am a sinner. I need forgiveness. But I am a Samaritan. You Jews tell me I have to worship in Jerusalem. How would that go over if I showed up at your temple?"

Jesus pointed out to her that God's salvation is from the Jews—that is, the promised Messiah would be a Jew; he would come from the family of King David. In fact, that's why God commanded the Jews to worship in Jerusalem. That's why he governed their worship life the way he had. All their worship, all their sacrifices, all their rituals and feasts, the temple itself— all of it pointed to the Messiah who would come. But once the Messiah came, once he paid for the sins of the whole world, such regulated worship of sacrifices, feasts and festivals, and even the temple itself will have served their purpose. They would no longer be necessary. The worship that the Lord would delight in would not be confined to a specific place or rite but to spirit and truth.

We worship God in spirit and truth. We worship God not just on the weekend at church and not just on Wednesday nights during Advent and Lent. We worship God—we serve him—24/7. Every day of our lives we have the privilege and opportunity to offer ourselves to God as living sacrifices. Everything we think, do, and say can show him our gratitude, love, devotion, and contentment. That we can do anywhere at any time.

*May all I do, Lord, be done to your glory and praise. Amen.*

# I Am He

**John 4:25,26**

*The woman said to him, "I know that Messiah is coming" (the one called Christ). "When he comes, he will explain everything to us."*
*Jesus said to her, "I, the one speaking to you, am he."*

Put yourself in this woman's shoes. Goosebumps, right? Shivers down the spine? She had been talking to this man who seemed to know so much about her—about her past, about her sins. She had been talking to this man who seemed to know so much about God—about worship, about truth, about the future. She professed her faith. She shared her hope. "I know that Messiah is coming. When he comes, he will explain everything to us."

"I, the one speaking to you, am he."

Wow!

Goosebumps.

Imagine: the one whom you had been waiting for—your Savior from sin, your spiritual Shepherd, the one promised to come—suddenly says to you (without you having any prior knowledge as to who this stranger is), "I am he." Imagine the shock. Imagine the joy. Imagine not being sure of what to do or say. "Christ is here, talking to me!"

The same Christ who spoke to this woman at the well, who pointed out her sin only to point out her Savior (himself!), speaks to us today. Christ comes to us in Word and sacrament to assure us that he is the one whom we have been waiting for. He is our Savior from sin, he is our spiritual Shepherd, and he is the one promised to come. In him we have forgiveness, life, and an eternal future.

Wow!

*Thank you, Jesus, for coming to me. Thank you for coming to me in Word and sacrament. Thank you for coming to me with your divine assurance of my forgiveness and salvation. Amen.*

---

## You Won't Believe This!

### John 4:27-30

> *Just then his disciples returned and were surprised that he was talking to a woman. Yet no one asked, "What do you want?" or "Why are you talking to her?"*
>
> *Then the woman left her water jar and went back into town. She said to the people, "Come, see the man who told me everything I ever did. Could this be the Christ?" They left the town and came to him.*

The disciples had gone into town to buy food. When they got back, Jesus and this woman were just finishing their conversation. Jesus had just told this woman that he was the promised Messiah! She ran. She ran not in shame. She ran not in fear of Jesus. She ran not in fear of this large group of men. She ran because she had good news—good news she just had to share. She ran to tell others about this conversation she just had, to tell others about this man with whom she had just spoken, that she may have just seen the Christ!

The people whom she told were curious. They were interested. They went to investigate. They went to see for themselves. Later, John will tell us that some of them believed!

Jesus died. Jesus rose. Jesus will come again. Those are the basics of the Christian faith. Jesus has told us this in his Word.

Because Jesus died and rose, he will take us to heaven when he comes again. Good news? News worth sharing? Any need to run—not in fear but in joy? To run and tell others that Jesus is the Christ?

You may be reading this at Christmas. You may be reading this during Lent. You may be reading this on Easter. It could be the middle of summer. It might be the end of fall. Regardless, we have opportunities every week to invite people to church. These people could be members of your own church who don't normally come; they could be family, friends, or coworkers who are confused, hurting, or straying; they could be total strangers who are searching for something but haven't been able to find it on their own. They all—as do we—need to drink again and again from the living water that wells up to eternal life. Public worship is one way for us to say to others, as this Samaritan woman said to the people back in town, "Come and see!"

*Bless my witnessing, Lord. As this Samaritan woman ran to tell others about Jesus, help me run with the same joy and sense of urgency as I share with others what you did to save the world from sin. Amen.*

---

## The Harvest Is Ripe

**John 4:31-38**

*Meanwhile, the disciples kept urging him, "Rabbi, eat."*
*But Jesus said to them, "I have food to eat that you do not know about."*
*Then the disciples said to each other, "Did anyone bring him something to eat?"*

*Jesus told them, "My food is to do the will of him who sent me and to finish his work. Do you not say, 'Four more months and the harvest will be here'? Pay attention to what I am telling you. Open your eyes and look at the fields because they are already ripe for harvest. The reaper is getting paid and is gathering grain for eternal life, so that the sower and the reaper may rejoice together. Indeed in this case the saying is true, 'One sows, and another reaps.' I sent you to reap a harvest for which you did no hard work. Others have done the hard work, and you have benefitted from their labor."*

Have you ever experienced how frustrating and discouraging it can be, at times, to continually plant seeds in the hearts of people around you but to never see any fruit? Maybe you have a handful of people in your life to whom you have been witnessing and with whom you have been sharing your Savior but with very little success. That's the "hard work" Jesus spoke about in the verses above—planting the seed of the Word. It's hard work because we don't always see the harvest. We may never see or hear that person confess faith in Christ, but that doesn't mean that this person will never confess faith in Christ. At just the right time in that person's life, God may use another Christian's witnessing to bring that person to faith. It's like when a parent takes a young child fishing, doing all the hard work of getting a fish on the line and getting that fish hooked only to have the child do the easy work—the fun work—of reeling in the fish.

Jesus was telling his disciples that the harvest was ripe—the spiritual harvest among both the Samaritans and the Jews was ripe. Others had done the hard work—Moses and other Old Testament prophets, John the Baptist, Jesus, even this Samaritan woman. Now the disciples were going to reap the benefits of the sown seed—they would get to reel in the fish as they came out to the well to see Jesus.

Whether we are sowing or reaping, whether we are casting or reeling in, know that the harvest is ripe, we have the sickle of the gospel, and God will use us to gather his elect.

*"Hark! The voice of Jesus crying, 'Who will go and work today? Fields are ripe and harvests waiting; who will bear the sheaves away?'" Lord, help me answer, "Here am I; send me, send me." Amen.*

---

## The Word Works

### John 4:39-42

*Many Samaritans from that town believed in him because of the woman's testimony: "He told me everything I ever did." So when the Samaritans came to him, they asked him to stay with them. And he stayed there two days. Many more believed because of his message. They told the woman, "We no longer believe because of what you said. Now we have heard for ourselves. And we know that this really is the Savior of the world."*

God's Word works. God's Word, shared by the Samaritan woman, worked—it brought these Samaritans out to see Jesus. God's Word worked—it moved these people to listen to Jesus. God's Word worked—it caused these people to want to hear more of it: "Stay longer!" God's Word worked—not only did it increase their knowledge of their Savior, but it also strengthened their faith in that Savior. God's Word worked—it moved the people to publicly confess their faith in Jesus.

God's Word works. It works when we share it. It works when it prompts us to go to church and stay for Bible class. It works when it creates in us a desire to hear more of it. It works as it increases our knowledge and strengthens our faith. It works when it moves us to publicly confess our faith in Jesus. The truth is, we need it. We need it to grow in our desire to hear the Word, in our knowledge of the Word, in our faith, and in our confidence in sharing the Word—all of us do. The Word makes that all happen. The Word works.

*Holy Spirit, continue to bless your Word whenever I read, hear, study, or share it. Strengthen my faith. Increase my knowledge. Empower me to respond. Guide me in my living. Amen.*

---

# What Do You Want out of Jesus?

### John 4:43-54

*After two days, Jesus left for Galilee. Now Jesus himself had testified that a prophet is not honored in his own country.*

*When he came to Galilee, the Galileans welcomed him. They had seen all the things he did at the Festival in Jerusalem, because they also had gone to the Festival.*

*Jesus came again to Cana in Galilee, where he had turned the water into wine.*

*In Capernaum, there was a certain royal official whose son was sick. When this man heard that Jesus had come*

*from Judea into Galilee, he went to him and begged him*
*to come down and heal his son, because his son was*
*about to die.*

*Jesus told him, "Unless you people see miraculous signs*
*and wonders, you certainly will not believe."*

*The royal official said to him, "Lord, come down before*
*my little boy dies."*

*"Go," Jesus told him, "your son is going to live."*

*The man believed this word that Jesus spoke to him*
*and left.*

*Already as he was going down, his servants met*
*him with the news that his boy was going to live. So he*
*asked them what time his son got better. They told him,*
*"Yesterday at the seventh hour the fever left him." Then*
*the father realized that was the exact time when Jesus*
*had told him, "Your son is going to live." And he himself*
*and his whole household believed.*

*This was the second miraculous sign Jesus did after he*
*came from Judea into Galilee.*

The Samaritans had honored Jesus—they believed his message. The people in Galilee, while Jesus had impressed and amazed them, did not honor him—they did not believe his message. They followed him, they went to him, not because they wanted to hear and learn more, not because they saw him as their Savior from sin but because they saw him as a miracle worker and simply as someone who could help them out of a jam. See the patient way that Jesus dealt with this royal official whose son was sick. Jesus didn't hesitate to rebuke either him or the crowd. He told the official to take him at his word. Jesus didn't go with him or give him a sign. Jesus didn't do anything. He simply told him that his son would live; Jesus was calling this official to trust him and his word. That trust was not misplaced. His son was healed at that very moment.

An account like this one forces us to pause and reflect and ask ourselves just what it is we want out of Jesus. Are we content and satisfied to have him as our Savior from sin? Or do we turn to him, nine times out of ten, for help out of this jam or that, asking for help with a job, bill, sickness, or relationship? Please understand that God invites us to call on him in the day of trouble (Psalm 50:15)—that passage even goes on to say that we will honor him when we do. But let us also be careful that we don't turn Jesus into just that—someone we turn to only when we need help in this life (like the people in Galilee were doing). First and foremost, Jesus is our Savior from sin. First and foremost, Jesus would have us come to him with prayers regarding our spiritual lives, our faith in him, and our struggles against temptation. Jesus would have us regularly confess our sins and turn to him for forgiveness. Jesus wants us to turn to him for strength and guidance in our roles as parents, spouses, children, students, employees, friends, neighbors, or church leaders.

We can go to Jesus with any request, but first and foremost, let us honor him with requests that acknowledge him as our Savior from sin.

*Forgive me, Jesus, for my earth-minded focus and prayers. Help me to set my mind on things above and not on earthly things. May all my prayers honor you. Amen.*

# Walk!

## John 5:1-9

*After this, there was a Jewish festival, and Jesus went up to Jerusalem.*

*Near the Sheep Gate in Jerusalem there is a pool, called Bethesda in Aramaic, which has five colonnades. Within these lay a large number of sick people—blind, lame, or paralyzed—who were waiting for the movement of the water. For an angel would go down at certain times into the pool and stir up the water. Whoever stepped in first after the stirring of the water was healed of whatever disease he had. One man was there who had been sick for thirty-eight years. When Jesus saw him lying there and knew he had already been sick a long time, he asked him, "Do you want to get well?"*

*"Sir," the sick man answered, "I have no one to put me into the pool when the water is stirred up. While I'm going, someone else goes down ahead of me."*

*Jesus said to him, "Get up! Pick up your mat and walk." Instantly the man was healed. He picked up his mat and walked.*

Some would like to know more about this pool near the Sheep Gate in Jerusalem. Did its water really bring healing? Who "stirred" this water—was it an angel? Was this a magical pool and were the people around it superstitious? How many people over the years had been healed there? Was only the first person into the pool, after the water was stirred, healed? Was God behind the healing?

John records this account, however, not so that we will focus on the pool or its water but so that we will focus on Jesus and his almighty power as the Son of God. See how powerful his Word was—"Get up," and the man was healed. After 38 years of not even being able to get himself into the pool, not only could this man now get up, but he could also pick up his mat and walk.

What can Jesus do for us? Anything, really. Anything we ask. Anything that is in line with his will. But as we consider the end of chapter 4, while we can pray for anything, while Jesus invites us to call upon him in the day of trouble and cast all our anxiety on him, first and foremost his will is that he, our Savior, wants all to be saved and come to a knowledge of the truth, all people to repent, and for us to grow in our faith and understanding. What can Jesus do for us? Look at what he has already done for us! He already brought us to faith. He already washed away our sins. He empowers us daily to repent. He sends his Holy Spirit through Word and sacrament to strengthen our faith and even increase our knowledge. Far greater than giving us the physical ability to get up and walk, Jesus has raised us from spiritual death and has given us the legs of faith to live a life of love. If there is some physical blessing along the way that Jesus knows will help us on our walk of faith, we can be sure that he can and will give it.

*Holy Spirit, strengthen my faith in Jesus through Word and sacrament. Remind me daily that the all-powerful God who did not spare his own Son but gave him up for me can certainly, along with him, graciously give me all things. Amen.*

# Who Did This?

### John 5:9-14

*That day was the Sabbath. So the Jews told the man who had been healed, "This is the Sabbath! You are not permitted to carry your mat."*

*He answered them, "The one who made me well told me, 'Pick up your mat and walk.'"*

*Then they asked him, "Who is the man who told you, 'Pick it up and walk'?" But the man who was healed did not know who it was, for Jesus had slipped away into the crowd that was there.*

*Later Jesus found him in the temple and said to him, "Look, you are well now. Do not sin anymore so that nothing worse happens to you."*

The actual Sabbath laws of the Old Testament forbad people to work on the Sabbath, but they did not forbid a man from picking up a mat or walking home. (They certainly did not forbid the Son of God to heal on the Sabbath.) These additional rules and regulations—a person can walk only so many paces on the Sabbath, defining work as something other than doing those things that helped you earn a living—were brought in later by the Pharisees. The Pharisees added hundreds of rules and regulations to God's Old Testament laws—rules they could actually keep; rules that set them above the rest of the people who didn't keep them; rules they believed would enable them, in their work-righteousness, to earn favor with God and even their own eternal salvation.

So neither this man nor Jesus sinned on the Sabbath, but the Pharisees felt compelled to investigate. They wanted to shake a condemning finger at the one responsible for this travesty. The man didn't know who had healed him until Jesus found him in the temple. Jesus offered this man a spiritual warning—a call to repentance. He told him to stop sinning, or something worse may happen to him. This warning of Jesus can best be taken this way: to stop sinning means to live a life of repentance. No one can stop sinning, but the child of God can confess his or her sins, trust in God for forgiveness, and turn from those sins in the future. "Or something worse may happen" means that those who die living a life of impenitent sin will die eternally in hell (rather than implying that some sin of this man had caused his previous handicap and now he had to guard against a greater sin and handicap).

God wants us to live lives of repentance. Repentance isn't something we do once in our lives and then we're done. Repentance isn't something we do once a week. Daily we drown our old Adam in contrition and repentance so that daily a new person may arise as from the dead. Daily we see, acknowledge, and confess our sins; daily we turn to Jesus for forgiveness, trusting that his death paid for our sins and all is well with God; daily we fight against temptation; and daily we avoid those situations where we know we will be tempted.

*Thank you, Lord, for the gift of faith that receives your forgiveness and your spiritual healing. Help me now, every day, to live my life for you. Amen.*

# God Doesn't Rest

**John 5:15-18**

> *The man went back and reported to the Jews that it was Jesus who made him well.*
>
> *So the Jews began to persecute Jesus because he was doing these things on the Sabbath. But Jesus answered them, "My Father is working right up to the present time, and I am working too."*
>
> *This is why the Jews tried all the more to kill him, because he was not merely breaking the Sabbath, but was even calling God his own Father, making himself equal with God.*

We don't need to assume that the reason this man went to tell the Jews that Jesus was the one who had healed him was because he wanted to get Jesus in trouble or because he was aware of their hatred toward Jesus or because he was interested in taking sides in all this. Rather, putting the best construction on this, this man may have simply gone to tell the Jews who it was who had healed him because he wanted to give credit where credit was due. He wanted to praise God to his religious leaders for this miraculous healing.

The Jewish leaders did not join him in his thanksgiving and praise. Rather, they set out to persecute Jesus. They questioned him. They wanted not merely to silence him but to eliminate him altogether. Things only intensified when Jesus called God his Father, when he indicated that he and his Father are always working, and when he basically made himself equal with God the Father. The Jewish leaders didn't want to hear that; they didn't want to believe that; they wouldn't accept that.

But what a great reminder for us! "My Father is always at work to this very day!" God the Father doesn't take a day off. God the

Father doesn't sleep. God the Father doesn't go off on vacation. And neither does Jesus! They are always at work—guarding and protecting us, caring and providing for us, helping and blessing us, healing and comforting us, guiding and directing us. Never will this world spin out of control. Never will our lives spin out of control. Never do we need to fear or worry that God will ever stop holding us in the palm of his hand.

*Heavenly Father, comfort and bless all those who are sad, troubled, confused, lonely, and afraid with your gracious promise of eternal life in Christ. Amen.*

## You Ain't Seen Nothing Yet

### John 5:19-23

*Jesus answered them directly, "Amen, Amen, I tell you: The Son can do nothing on his own, but only what he sees the Father doing. Indeed, the Son does exactly what the Father does. For the Father loves the Son and shows him everything he is doing. And he will show him even greater works than these so that you will be amazed. For just as the Father raises the dead and gives them life, so also the Son gives life to those he wishes.*

*"In fact, the Father judges no one, but has entrusted all judgment to the Son, so that all should honor the Son just as they honor the Father. Whoever does not honor the Son does not honor the Father who sent him."*

The Jewish religious leaders were upset that Jesus had made himself equal with God the Father. Jesus had indeed done that because he is equal with God the Father—they are both God, both holy, both eternal, both all-powerful, both all-knowing, both present everywhere. But Jesus had also humbled himself; he did not consider equality with God something to be grasped. He made himself nothing; he took on human flesh. According to his human nature, Jesus submitted himself to the will of God—he would do whatever the Father does, whatever the Father would have him do.

And what would God have him do? Live a perfect life of obedience in our place. Suffer the punishment of hell in our place. Die in our place. Rise from the dead to assure us of our free salvation and inheritance of eternal life. Ascend into heaven as the glorified Son of God who now rules all things for the good of his church and the good of his people. And he will come again to judge. All this work God the Father entrusted to his Son. At the time of his conversation with the religious leaders, much of this work was still to come. In a sense Jesus was telling them, "You ain't seen nothing yet. If you think this healing of an invalid is something, if you think equating myself with God the Father is something, wait until I suffer hell on the cross, rise from the dead, ascend into heaven, and return in glory to judge the living and the dead—then you'll see something. Then every knee will bow, and every tongue will confess that I am the Lord."

*Thank you, Holy Spirit, for this brief glimpse into the inner workings of the Trinity and the truth that Jesus is both true God and true man in one person. Though these things will never make logical sense to my rational mind, enable my faith to embrace them as truth and rely on all of you—Father, Son, and Holy Spirit—for my eternal salvation. Amen.*

# Do Not Be Amazed at This

### John 5:24-30

*"Amen, Amen, I tell you: Anyone who hears my word and believes him who sent me has eternal life. He is not going to come into judgment but has crossed over from death to life.*

*"Amen, Amen, I tell you: A time is coming and is here now when the dead will hear the voice of the Son of God, and those who listen will live. For just as the Father has life in himself, so also he has granted the Son to have life in himself. And he has given him authority to execute judgment, because he is the Son of Man.*

*"Do not be amazed at this, for a time is coming when all who are in their graves will hear his voice and will come out. Those who have done good will rise to live, but those who have practiced evil will rise to be condemned. I can do nothing at all on my own. I judge only as I hear. And my judgment is just, for I do not seek my own will, but the will of him who sent me."*

Jesus is life. Jesus gives life.

Jesus gives spiritual life through his Word. He made us spiritually alive when, through his Word, he gave us the faith to believe in him as our Savior.

Jesus will also give back physical life through that same powerful Word. When he returns to judge the living and the dead, all who are in their graves will hear his voice and come out.

At that time, Jesus will give eternal life to all who heard his Word and believed that God the Father had sent him to live and die and rise again.

As Jesus judges the world on the Last Day, he will base that judgment on one criterion and one criterion alone—faith or no faith. Those who believe in him will be saved; those who do not believe in him will be condemned. How will Jesus confirm this judgment? How will Jesus identify those who believe and those who do not believe? He will point to their works, to their deeds. Those who have done good—through the faith Jesus gave them—will live eternally with him (not because they did good but because the good they did gave evidence of their faith in him). Those who have not done good—those who insisted on living as they pleased—will die eternally without him (their evil deeds will serve as evidence against them that they did not believe in him).

*Thank you, thank you, thank you, Jesus, for giving me life—for the spiritual life I have now to know, believe, and trust in you (and also live for you!); the physical life you will give back to me on the Last Day at the great resurrection of all the dead; and the eternal life in the world to come, which you will give freely to all who believe in you. Amen.*

---

## Witness #1

### John 5:31-35

*"If I were to testify about myself, my testimony would not be valid. There is another who testifies about me, and I know that his testimony about me is valid. You sent to John, and he has testified to the truth. The testimony I receive is not from man, but I am saying these things so that you may be saved. John was a lamp that was shining brightly, and for a while you wanted to enjoy his light."*

Jesus had been making some pretty big claims. He had claimed that God the Father had sent him into the world. He had claimed that he was the Son of God. He had claimed that he and the Father were equal. He had claimed that the Father had entrusted him with not only saving the world but also judging the world. Some pretty big claims coming from only one source—his own mouth.

In a Jewish court of law and in the Old Testament Scriptures, it was clear that every matter needed to be settled by the testimony of two or three witnesses. Though Jesus readily acknowledged that he, as the Son of God, did not need any witnesses to legitimize his claims, he would substantiate his claims nonetheless by the witness and testimony of two or three others. He did this for their sake so that they may believe in him.

His first witness was John the Baptist—the one who had come before him, the one whom he had surpassed, the one who was not worthy to untie his sandals, the one who had pointed to him and said, "Look! The Lamb of God, who takes away the sin of the world!" John's message—which even the Jews had believed and accepted for a time—confirmed and substantiated Jesus' claims.

The testimony of John the Baptist is for our benefit as well. The Holy Spirit still works today through the message of John to prepare hearts for Jesus and point our eyes of faith to the Lamb of God, Jesus Christ, who has taken away our sin. Jesus was not a liar. He was not a renegade making bold and unsubstantiated claims about himself. He is the Son of God and our Savior from sin. There's no doubt about that.

*Holy Spirit, thank you for the testimony of John about Jesus. Eliminate all doubt from my heart. Enable me to trust solely in Jesus as my Savior from sin. Amen.*

# Witness #2

## John 5:36-40

*"But I have testimony greater than John's. For the works that the Father gave me to carry out, the very works that I am doing, these testify about me that the Father has sent me. The Father who sent me—he is the one who has testified about me. You have never heard his voice or seen his form. And you do not have his word remaining in you, because you do not believe the one he sent. You search the Scriptures because you think you have eternal life in them. They testify about me! And yet you do not want to come to me in order to have life."*

Though he had no personal need to substantiate his divine claims, for the sake of those who were listening to him and so they might believe him, Jesus was in the middle of offering the two or three witnesses who could establish the matter. Jesus was telling them, "Don't take my word for it. Look at John the Baptist. He told you who I am. He told you I was sent by God the Father. He told you I am the Lamb of God."

His second witness? None other than God the Father. From the night of Jesus' birth when God the Father sent a sky full of angels to announce the peace that would come through the birth of his Son into the world to his baptism in the Jordan River when God the Father spoke—even to the Mount of Transfiguration account still to come and to the silence of the empty tomb that would proclaim him to be his Son—God the Father had testified that Jesus is his Son, he is his equal, his work is the same as his, and his authority is the same as his.

These religious leaders thought they knew the Word of God. And, to be sure, they did know it. They had read it. They had studied it. They had memorized it. They knew the letter of the law. But through that Word they did not have life, either spiritual or eternal, because in its pages they did not see Jesus Christ, the Son of God, the promised Messiah. They did not see Jesus as the fulfillment of what they knew of the Old Testament.

By God's grace we possess eternal life through the Scriptures because the Holy Spirit has given us the eyes of faith to see Christ on every page. The key to understanding the Scriptures is to read it in the light of Jesus. He is the one to whom all Scripture points—the Old Testament pointing forward, the New Testament pointing backward. The purpose of the Bible is not to make us morally good people. The purpose of the Bible is what John will say in chapter 20:31—"These are written that you may believe that Jesus is the Christ, the Son of God, and that by believing you may have life [spiritual and eternal life] in his name."

*Thank you, heavenly Father, for sharing your Son with the world—both through his incarnation, life, and death and also through your Word so that I may believe in him and have life. Amen.*

---

## Whose Praise Is Whose?

### John 5:41-44

*"I do not accept honor from people. But I know you. I know that you do not have the love of God within you. I have come in my Father's name, yet you do not accept me. If someone else comes in his own name, you will accept him. How can you believe while you continue to accept glory from one another and you do not seek the glory that comes from the only God?"*

Jesus knew why these religious leaders did not believe him—they weren't in this for the right reasons. They hadn't immersed themselves in God's Word, they didn't live pious lives, and they didn't devote themselves to temple worship rites for God but for themselves. Their goal was not to praise God. Their goal was not even to receive praise from God. Their goal was to receive praise from each other. It's no wonder they didn't love God—they loved themselves. It's no wonder they didn't serve God—they served themselves. It's no wonder they didn't trust in Jesus—they put their trust in themselves.

God forgive our arrogance! God forgive our self-praise! God forgive our self-service!

And he does!

He does because Jesus humbled himself and became obedient to death. He does because Jesus' life of obedience (lived in our place!) brought praise, honor, and glory to God. He does because Jesus served us and the whole world by giving his life as a ransom for us.

*Lord, empower, enable, and motivate me to serve you and others with a humble attitude that does all things to your glory. Amen.*

## Judged by the Law

### John 5:45-47

*"Do not think that I will accuse you to the Father. The one who accuses you is Moses, on whom you have set your hope. For if you believed Moses, you would believe me, because he wrote about me. But if you do not believe his writings, how will you believe what I say?"*

These religious leaders took pride in knowing the books of Moses: the first five books of the Old Testament. They took pride in obeying the laws of Moses. They took pride in knowing the Old Testament Scriptures, "for in them they thought they had life."

Jesus burst their bubble. If only they knew Moses! If only they read the books of Moses in the light of Christ! If only they saw the laws of Moses pointing to their ultimate fulfillment in Christ! The fact was that the one person whom they prided themselves on knowing and following was now their accuser. Moses, the lawgiver, would condemn them for their unbelief; he would condemn them for their refusal to acknowledge that Jesus was the Son of God. The law they prided themselves on keeping would judge and condemn them.

Moses will not condemn us. Moses will not judge us. The law will not condemn us. The law will not judge us. Christ has fulfilled the requirements of the law in our place. God has credited his righteousness to us by faith in Christ, which he has given us. For us who are in Christ, there is now no condemnation. Freed from the law, we now use the law as a guide in our lives of faith, love, and thanksgiving.

*Thank you, Holy Spirit, for the eyes of faith that enable me to see my Savior on every page of the Old Testament. Amen.*

# How Will We Do This?

## John 6:1-6

*After this, Jesus crossed over to the other side of the Sea of Galilee (or Tiberias). A large crowd followed him because they saw the miraculous signs he was performing on those who were sick. Jesus went up on the hillside and sat down there with his disciples. The Jewish Passover Festival was near.*

*When Jesus looked up and saw a huge crowd coming toward him, he asked Philip, "Where can we buy bread for these people to eat?" But Jesus was saying this to test him, for he himself knew what he was going to do.*

As unpopular as Jesus was with the Jewish religious leaders, his popularity with the Jewish people was only growing. Miracles of healing and help attracted large crowds. These crowds were even willing to follow him to the far shore of the Sea of Galilee where they sat down to listen to Jesus teach. These verses set the scene for John chapter 6—the chapter of the Bible known for the feeding of the five thousand and the Bread of Life discourse.

Jesus saw the crowds in front of him. The disciples saw the crowds in front of them. Both Jesus and the disciples knew it was getting late and these people would need to eat. But where would they find food? Where would they get food? This was the question Jesus asked Philip. Jesus knew where he was going to get food. Jesus knew he would miraculously feed this crowd of people. But did the disciples? Did Philip? They had seen many miracles to date. Did they trust that Jesus could provide for them and this large crowd? Did they think Jesus would have enough love and compassion—enough generosity—to provide a meal for all these people? We'll have to wait to hear Philip's answer and Jesus' response.

For now we simply ask, "What about us?" Do we trust that Jesus has enough love and compassion—enough generosity—to help us in our time of need? Do we trust that Jesus can provide for us and our families—regardless of the money we may have in the bank, regardless of what we may owe in taxes each year, regardless of the bills that are piling up, regardless of the retirement fund that is shrinking? "How will we do this?" we ask. His answer, in effect, is what Proverbs 3:5 teaches: "Trust in the LORD with all your heart, and do not rely on your own understanding." God's Word also teaches that if God did not spare his own Son but graciously gave him up for you and for your sins, how will he not also, along with him, graciously give you all things (see Romans 8:32).

*Give me a heart of faith, O Lord, that continually puts my trust in you and your love, compassion, and generosity, but, most of all, give me a faith that puts my trust in Jesus my Savior. Amen.*

---

# Jesus Feeds the Five Thousand
### John 6:7-11

> *Philip answered him, "Two hundred denarii worth of bread would not be enough for each of them to have just a little."*
>
> *One of his disciples, Andrew, Simon Peter's brother, said to him, "There's a boy here who has five barley loaves and two fish, but what is that for so many people?"*
>
> *Jesus said, "Have the people sit down." There was plenty of grass in that place, so they sat down. There were about five thousand men.*

*Then Jesus took the loaves and, after giving thanks, he distributed pieces to those who were seated. He also did the same with the fish—as much as they wanted.*

Philip didn't do so well with Jesus' test. Jesus had asked him where they could buy enough food to feed all the people. Philip didn't even suggest a place; he realized that even if there had been a place close by where they could buy food, the disciples wouldn't have had enough money to buy it. Andrew chimed in: "We have a boy here with his lunch—five loaves and two fish—but how far will that go?" While Philip and Andrew had failed Jesus' test, it did lead them to see that there was no human solution to the problem in front of them. But what about a divine solution?

Jesus took control. The people sat down—five thousand men. Just as many women? Just as many children? More children? Were there 15,000 people on that grassy hill? Could these people have filled a basketball arena? Yeah, probably. Picture that. And Jesus fed them all—with five loaves and two fish. He fed them all and they all had their fill—as much as they wanted. This was not a case of Jesus appealing to the crowd, "Look, here is a boy willing to share his lunch; what about you? Can we all find something that we brought along and share it so that all can have some?" No. This was a miracle. This miracle reveals that Jesus is the Son of God. This miracle reveals Jesus' generosity and care.

The tests that God gives us in life are never intended to make us fail. Rather, the tests that God gives us in life are intended to make us stronger. They make us stronger by forcing us to stop looking at ourselves and our own solutions and start looking at God and his solutions—and power. That's what Philip and Andrew learned; that's what Philip and Andrew would encourage us to do. No, that's what our caring, generous, almighty God would have us do.

*Heavenly Father, like Paul I confess that your grace is sufficient for me because I see that your power is made perfect in my weakness. Amen.*

---

# Leftovers

### John 6:12,13

> *When the people were full, he told his disciples, "Gather the pieces that are left over so that nothing is wasted." So they gathered them and filled twelve baskets with pieces from the five barley loaves left over by those who had eaten.*

One boy with his lunch—five loaves of bread and two small fish. That's what Jesus had started with. Jesus fed the five thousand—in reality, he fed far more than that—with a lunch meant for one boy. So well did he feed them that John tells us that everyone had his fill. They all ate and were satisfied. How could this be possible? With God nothing is impossible. With God all things are possible. Jesus is God. Jesus used his almighty power to perform this miracle. In the verses before us today, John emphasizes just how great this miracle was. Not only did everyone have his fill, but after the meal there was so much food left over that the disciples were able to gather 12 baskets full of food.

What do these leftovers show us? Yes, they show us Jesus' almighty power, but they also show us his generosity—Jesus had given the people more than they could eat. The leftovers also show us what it means to be a good steward. Jesus did not let this extra food go to waste. It could be served and eaten at a future meal. Those who had longer journeys home could even take some food with them on the road.

The same all-powerful God provides for us today. No, probably not through miracles such as this one, but certainly through the ability to work and earn an income that he gives us, certainly through his creation (seasons and crops and animals), certainly through the kindness and generosity of others. God would have us be wise stewards of all that he gives us. Here he wanted nothing to go to waste. Perhaps we can keep that in mind as we live thankful, content lives that acknowledge him as the giver of every good and perfect gift.

*I thank you, heavenly Father, for all that you give me day after day. I know that I am not worthy of anything you have given me. I pray that you would enable me to receive my daily bread with thanksgiving and use all you give me wisely and to your glory. Amen.*

---

## A Bread King?

### John 6:14,15

*When the people saw the miraculous sign Jesus did, they said, "This really is the Prophet who is coming into the world."*
*When Jesus realized that they intended to come and take him by force to make him king, he withdrew again to the mountain by himself.*

Jesus displayed his almighty power as the Son of God by feeding this large group of people with such a small amount of food.

These people saw Jesus as the second coming of Moses. They saw in Jesus another man who could feed them and take care of them and make life easy—just as Moses had provided manna and quail and water in the desert, though God was the one who had actually done that. They wanted to make Jesus their bread king. They were willing to give him worship, honor, and praise; they were willing to give him loyalty, obedience, and support. All he had to do was take care of them with more of these miracles.

See the temptation before Jesus. Fame! Prestige! Honor! Influence! A huge following! He wouldn't have to suffer. He wouldn't have to die. He could just be their miracle-working bread king. Our promised Savior would have none of it! And thank him that he didn't! He withdrew again by himself. He fled the temptation. He looked to his Father for strength. He stayed the course. He was determined to walk to the cross to pay for our sins. Our Savior! Willing. Determined. Obedient. Faithful. Loving. He gave us something far better than a miraculous meal. He gave us the forgiveness of sins and the right to eat at God's eternal wedding banquet.

*Lord Jesus Christ, in my life of faith, empower me to give you the honor, praise, and glory that you deserve as my Savior-King. Amen.*

# It Is I. Do Not Be Afraid

### John 6:16-21

*When evening came, his disciples went down to the sea, got into a boat, and started across the sea to Capernaum. It was already dark, and Jesus had not yet come to them. A strong wind started to blow, and the sea became rough.*

*After they had rowed about three or four miles, they saw Jesus walking on the sea toward their boat, and they were afraid.*

*But he said to them, "It is I. Do not be afraid!"*

*Then they were willing to take him into the boat, and immediately the boat reached the shore where they were heading.*

To set the stage—Jesus just miraculously fed the five thousand. The people wanted to make Jesus their bread king. Jesus saw this as a temptation not to go through with the suffering and death necessary to pay for the sins of the world. Jesus fled the temptation; he withdrew to a nearby mountain by himself. Before doing so, he had told the disciples to head back to the other side of the lake. Perhaps they assumed that he would walk around the lake and meet them later on the other side.

On the lake, the waters grew rough. The disciples, who were experienced sailors, battled the wind and waves. By early morning (between 3:00 A.M. and 6:00 A.M.), they had gotten only halfway across the lake. That's when they looked up and saw Jesus walking on the water! But they were afraid; they thought he was a ghost.

Notice what brought peace—the words of Jesus: "It is I. Do not be afraid." It was the Lord. It was the Son of God. It was their Savior. His words brought them peace. His words also calmed the storm—the wind and the waves. His words also brought them immediately and safely to the other side of the lake. Three more miracles! Jesus walked on water; Jesus calmed the storm; Jesus instantaneously brought the boat to the other side of the lake.

In his Word, Jesus says the same to you and me: "It is I. Do not be afraid." The same Jesus who fed the five thousand, walked on water, calmed the storm, and brought the boat to the other side of the lake is the same Jesus who knows our fears, troubles, and needs and promises to help—and there is no problem he cannot fix! How do we know? Look at the cross. Look at the empty tomb. Look at our status before God. We are holy and blameless before God. In spite of our sin, we are holy and blameless before God—because of Jesus and through faith in Jesus.

*Lord Jesus, strengthen my faith with the words you spoke to the disciples, "It is I. Do not be afraid." Amen.*

---

## Where's Jesus?

### John 6:22-24

> *The next day, the crowd that stayed on the other side of the sea noticed that only one boat was there. They also knew that Jesus had not stepped into the boat with his disciples, but they had gone away without him. Other boats from Tiberias came to shore near the place where they ate the bread after the Lord gave thanks. When the crowd saw that neither Jesus nor his disciples were there, they got into the boats and went to Capernaum looking for Jesus.*

After Jesus fed the five thousand, he went off by himself to pray—he avoided the temptation before him to be the miracle-working bread king of the people. It was at that time that the disciples got into their boat and set sail for the western side of the Sea of Galilee. The people? The crowd? They stayed overnight right there on the eastern side of the lake. When they woke up in the morning, they assumed that they would see Jesus. Only his disciples had gotten into the boat and left the night before, not Jesus. But Jesus wasn't around. They didn't know where he was. They wanted to find him, so when the boats from Tiberias arrived (a town on the western shore of the Sea of Galilee), they got in and set sail for Capernaum—hoping to find him there.

We know where to find Jesus today. We find him in Word and sacrament. We find him in the gospel. In fact, in the gospel he comes to us with his reassuring message of forgiveness and peace. In a world of uncertainty and change, in a world of hurt and heartache, in a world of sickness and disease, in a world of financial ups and downs, we find ourselves in need of constancy, comfort, encouragement, and reassuring peace. Where and where alone can we find such peace and confidence? In Christ. In Christ alone. Where do we find Christ? In his gospel. In his Word. In his sacraments. So where will we be? In worship. In Bible study. In his Word at home. There he gives us his peace and assures us of our eternal salvation.

*Lord Jesus, keep me connected to you, the vine, by keeping me in your Word. Amen.*

## Just Believe

### John 6:25-27

*When they found him on the other side of the sea, they asked him, "Rabbi, when did you get here?"*

*Jesus answered them, "Amen, Amen, I tell you: You are not looking for me because you saw the miraculous signs, but because you ate the loaves and were filled. Do not continue to work for the food that spoils, but for the food that endures to eternal life, which the Son of Man will give you. For on him God the Father has placed his seal of approval."*

Another quick recap—Jesus fed the five thousand; the disciples left by boat alone; Jesus walked on water; the crowd stayed overnight thinking they would see Jesus in the morning; they did not, so they set sail for the other side of the lake where they found him and asked him when he had gotten there.

Jesus didn't answer their question; instead, he addressed a greater need. He began what many have called his Bread of Life discourse—something we will consider together in the pages that follow. The miraculous feeding of the five thousand and the crowd's quest for more of the same is the backdrop for Jesus teaching them about spiritual bread, feeding their faith, and a spiritual food—the Word of God—that brings, offers, and provides eternal life.

Physical bread can sustain physical life. Spiritual bread sustains spiritual life. The crowd who followed Jesus across the lake needed to see that spiritual bread and spiritual life were far more important and far more valuable than any lunch or dinner—regardless of the menu or the manner in which it was provided. Perhaps these words apply to our materialistic society. Perhaps these words apply to us. How hard don't we work for the things of this life? How much time, effort, and thought go into the things that will not last? On the flip side, can we honestly say that we have the same zeal and desire, that we put in the same amount of time and effort, or that our spiritual diet of Word and sacrament are on the same plane?

"Do not continue to work for the food that spoils, but for the food that endures to eternal life," Jesus said. "This is the work of God: that you believe in the one he sent" (John 6:29).

*Heavenly Father, forgive me for my selfishness. Forgive me for my misplaced priorities. Forgive me for bending my knee and giving my heart to the god of materialism. Restore me in Jesus. Assure me of the forgiveness I have in Jesus, who humbled himself for me. Remind me that though he was rich, he became poor so that I through his poverty might become rich. Help me see how wealthy I am every time I feed on the life-giving bread of his Word. Amen.*

## Need a Sign?

**John 6:28-31**

*So they said to him, "What should we do to carry out the works of God?"*

*Jesus answered them, "This is the work of God: that you believe in the one he sent."*

*Then they asked him, "So what miraculous sign are you going to do, that we may see it and believe you? What miraculous sign are you going to perform? Our fathers ate the manna in the wilderness, just as it is written, 'He gave them bread from heaven to eat.' "*

The main point of the previous verses, the main point of these verses, and the main point of Jesus' entire Bread of Life discourse is simply this: Faith comes from hearing the message and the message is heard through the Word of Christ (Romans 10:17). Jesus was encouraging this crowd to study his Word, to read it, and to hear it. Jesus knows that it is through the living and enduring Word of God that the Holy Spirit will work the faith to believe in him. Jesus knows that those who through this God-given faith believe in him will live with him forever in heaven.

There is no work involved. There is nothing for us to do. Even believing in the one whom God has sent—Jesus—is the work of the Holy Spirit in us. Faith is the gift of God. He enables us to believe, but this crowd wasn't listening. This crowd had eyes that were ever seeing but never perceiving. They still were wondering what they needed to do. They still were hoping for daily bread rather than spiritual nourishment. They still, even after being encouraged to believe, wanted a sign. They did not want to live by faith but by sight. Doesn't the request for a sign—even just the sign itself—undermine the faith, the trust, that Jesus was calling them to have? Not only that, but hadn't Jesus just given them a sign? Hadn't he just miraculously fed them the day before?

God has given us his gift of faith. God has enabled us to believe in Jesus. Through faith we receive his forgiveness and his righteousness. We are empowered to trust in him for all things. We are motivated to live for him and give him glory in all we do. And all this is the work of God.

*Holy Spirit, give me the faith always to believe in the one whom God has sent to be my Savior. May I always live by faith and not by sight. May I always trust in God for his forgiveness and all I need to keep my body and life. Amen.*

# The Bread of Life

## John 6:32-40

> Jesus said to them, "Amen, Amen, I tell you: Moses did not give you the bread from heaven, but my Father gives you the real bread from heaven. For the bread of God is the one who comes down from heaven and gives life to the world."
>
> "Sir," they said to him, "give us this bread all the time!"
>
> "I am the Bread of Life," Jesus told them. "The one who comes to me will never be hungry, and the one who believes in me will never be thirsty. But I said to you that you have also seen me, and you do not believe. Everyone the Father gives me will come to me, and the one who comes to me I will never cast out. For I have come down from heaven, not to do my will, but the will of him who sent me. And this is the will of him who sent me: that I should lose none of those he has given me, but raise them up on the Last Day. For this is the will of my Father: that everyone who sees the Son and believes in him may have eternal life. And I will raise him up on the Last Day."

What did the people want? They wanted literal, physical bread. They wanted miracles. They wanted Moses and his manna. They wanted easy street. They wanted Jesus to simply give them what they wanted when they wanted it.

What did Jesus want? He wanted to give them spiritual bread. He wanted the Holy Spirit to work the miracle of faith in their hearts. He wanted them to have him and his Word. He wanted them to have the golden streets of eternal life. He wanted to give them what they needed, knowing that they needed it now.

They missed the point. They, like the woman at the well who wanted Jesus' living water, missed the point. Jesus had something far greater to give them than physical food and physical life; he was trying to give them spiritual food—the Word about him—and spiritual life, which would result in eternal life.

Hungry? Spiritually hungry? Jesus has a steady diet of life-giving bread for us to eat in his Word. In worship, in Bible class, in these devotions, in family devotions, in personal Bible study, and in sharing Bible stories with our children, Jesus feeds our faith and keeps us spiritually alive. He gives us the faith to know, trust, and believe that he will raise us up on the Last Day.

*Lord Jesus, as I look forward to the eternal life you have prepared for me, I pray that you would keep me spiritually alive through the living bread of your life-giving Word. May I eat of it often. Amen.*

---

## God Is My Teacher

### John 6:41-47

*So the Jews started grumbling about him, because he said, "I am the bread that came down from heaven." They asked, "Isn't this Jesus, the son of Joseph, whose father and mother we know? So how can he say, 'I have come down from heaven'?"*

*Jesus answered them, "Stop grumbling among yourselves. No one can come to me unless the Father who sent me draws him. And I will raise him up on the Last Day. It is written in the Prophets, 'They will all be taught by God.' Everyone who listens to the Father and learns from him comes to me. I am not saying that anyone has seen the Father except the one who is from God. He is the one who has seen the Father. Amen, Amen, I tell you: The one who believes in me has eternal life."*

The goal of anyone who teaches God's Word is not to convince or persuade anyone to believe anything. The purpose of anyone who teaches God's Word is not to argue or debate anyone into the kingdom of God or a right understanding of his Word. The goal, the purpose—the job, if you will—of anyone who teaches God's Word is simply to present what God teaches in his Word and let the Holy Spirit take it from there. The Holy Spirit can shatter through unbelieving hearts, humanistic errors, and rational, logical approaches to his Word. Those who hear his Word may, however, insist on keeping up those walls that keep the Holy Spirit out—walls built with the bricks of humanism, reason, and logic.

But in the end, a pastor or a teacher or a fellow Christian is not the one teaching those classes—God is. God teaches us through his Word. God teaches us his Word through his Son whom he sent into the world. The crowds who had eaten their fill grumbled when they heard that Jesus of Nazareth, the carpenter's son, had been sent from heaven. They kept their walls up. But to those whose walls of unbelief the Holy Spirit shattered as they were taught by God himself, Jesus would give everlasting life. God has been and continues to be our teacher. God teaches us in his Word. Jesus comes to us in his Word. The Holy Spirit strengthens our faith in his Word. By God's grace, we have everlasting life.

*Thank you, Jesus, for teaching me about my sin, my lack of faith, my stubbornness, and my inability to come to you on my own and be saved. Thank you, Jesus, for teaching me in your Word that you are my Savior from sin in whom I am righteous through faith and in whom I am forgiven. Amen.*

## Living Bread

### John 6:48-52

*"I am the Bread of Life. Your fathers ate manna in the
wilderness, and they died. This is the bread that comes
down from heaven, so that anyone may eat it and not die.
I am the living bread which came down from heaven. If
anyone eats this bread, he will live forever. The bread that
I will give for the life of the world is my flesh."*

*At that, the Jews argued among themselves, "How can
this man give us his flesh to eat?"*

The bread that God had given the Israelites in the desert to
eat—manna—kept them alive, but eventually those Israelites
all died. Is that really the kind of bread this crowd should have
been craving and seeking—bread that could keep them alive
physically, for a time, but would one day do them no good
because one day they would all die physically? And yet, physical bread was exactly what they continued to seek and have in
mind as they listened to Jesus. How could this man give them
his flesh to eat?

That's a good question. Many would answer that Jesus gives
us his flesh to eat in the Sacrament of Holy Communion. True
enough. But in the context of these verses, Jesus is not talking
about Communion. For one, he hadn't instituted it yet. Second,
Communion isn't for all people—it is for those who have been
instructed and can examine themselves. The scope of eating his
flesh is much larger than the Sacrament of Holy Communion.
The scope of eating his flesh—the living bread that came down
from heaven, the life that Jesus gave up for the world—is so
large that it is for all people. Jesus wants all people to eat his
flesh. Simply put, Jesus wants all people to hear his Word and
believe it. In the context of John chapter 6, eating Jesus' flesh

simply means believing that Jesus gave his flesh for our sin. All who believe this, all who by faith digest his Word, will have eternal life.

Bread worth eating? The manna gave physical life—but only for a time. The living bread that came down from heaven gives spiritual life—life that will last an eternity.

*Thank you, Jesus, for the sacrifice you made on the cross—your own flesh for my sin! Thank you for the spiritual diet of life-giving bread that you give me in your Word. May it strengthen me on the way that leads to eternal life. Amen.*

## Believe in His Sacrifice

### John 6:53-56

*So Jesus said to them, "Amen, Amen, I tell you: Unless you eat the flesh of the Son of Man and drink his blood, you do not have life in yourselves. The one who eats my flesh and drinks my blood has eternal life, and I will raise him up on the Last Day. For my flesh is real food, and my blood is real drink. The one who eats my flesh and drinks my blood remains in me, and I in him."*

Jesus continued his Bread of Life discourse, and those who were listening to him continued to take him literally. We ended our last devotion with the people asking, "How can this man give us his flesh to eat?" We noted then that eating Jesus' flesh simply meant believing in him as the one and only sacrifice for sin. Not trying to turn their stomachs any further but wanting them to stop thinking literally, Jesus now added the phrase "the one who . . . drinks my blood has eternal life." As we mentioned last time, this eating of flesh and drinking of blood are not literal, nor are they even a reference to the Lord's Supper—that hadn't been instituted yet. Rather, just as eating his flesh means believing in him as the one and only sacrifice for sin, so also drinking his blood means trusting that the blood he shed on the cross washes away all sin.

All those who believe that Jesus Christ came in the flesh, sacrificed his innocent flesh, and shed his holy blood on the cross to pay for all sin receive God's free and complete forgiveness. All those who believe in Jesus—that is, as Jesus said, all those who eat his flesh and drink his blood—will live forever in heaven. It's that simple. Thank God the Holy Spirit for the faith to digest such a simple gospel truth.

*Lord Jesus, I cannot thank you enough for giving yourself on the cross to pay for my sin. Holy Spirit, I cannot thank you enough for the faith in Jesus you have given me and continue to strengthen. Amen.*

---

## Life

### John 6:57-59

*"Just as the living Father sent me and I live because of the Father, so the one who feeds on me will live because of me. This is the bread that came down from heaven, not like your fathers ate and died. The one who eats this bread will live forever."*

*He said these things while teaching in the synagogue in Capernaum.*

We have life in Jesus. We have life in the one who lived in our place. We have life in the one who died in our place. We have life in the one who defeated death in our place by his own resurrection from the dead.

We have spiritual life already now. We are alive in Jesus. He is the living bread that came down from heaven. We who believe in him are spiritually alive. We have his gifts of faith, forgiveness, and righteousness. We have been empowered to live for him, serve him, and love him as we live for, serve, and love our neighbor.

We have eternal life yet to come. Jesus will raise us up on the Last Day. We will not die but live. We will live with Jesus forever in heaven—not because of us but because of him. As much as our heavenly Father gives us our daily bread, Jesus gives us himself, the living bread, so that we may eat it (believe in him) and not die.

*I thank you, God, for life—for my physical life that you continue to sustain, my spiritual life that keeps me in your family, and my eternal life that Jesus won for me. Amen.*

## A Hard Teaching

### John 6:60-66

*When they heard it, many of his disciples said, "This is a hard teaching! Who can listen to it?"*

*But Jesus, knowing in himself that his disciples were grumbling about this, asked them, "Does this cause you to stumble in your faith? What if you would see the Son of Man ascending to where he was before? The Spirit is the one who gives life. The flesh does not help at all. The words that I have spoken to you are spirit and they are life. But there are some of you who do not believe." For Jesus knew from the beginning those who would not believe and the one who would betray him. He said, "This is why I told you that no one can come to me unless it is given to him by my Father."*

*After this, many of his disciples turned back and were not walking with him anymore.*

The Bread of Life discourse was hard for this crowd of disciples to digest. It was difficult for them to stomach. Why? Because they were trying to digest this spiritual truth with the wisdom and reason of their flesh. No human being on his own can understand the spiritual truths of Scripture. The gospel does not make logical sense. Believing in Jesus as the only Savior from sin goes contrary to every proud bone in the human body. This teaching about the Bread of Life that came down from heaven offended this group so much that many of them turned back and stopped following Jesus.

Oh, how we can thank God for his gift of faith! Only a heart of faith can digest a spiritual message from the Bread of Life. Only the eyes of faith can see Jesus as the living bread who came down from heaven. Only the hand of faith can receive the forgiveness of sins and eternal life in heaven. The Spirit has given us this faith, this life, this hope, this knowledge, and this understanding. The Spirit has given us what we never could have attained on our own. The Father has enabled us not simply to come to Jesus but also, now, to follow Jesus as the Bread of Life, our only source of spiritual and eternal life.

*I thank you, Holy Spirit, for working through the means of grace—the gospel in both Word and sacrament. Continue to feed my faith with the life-giving bread of Jesus Christ. Amen.*

# Not You Too?

## John 6:67-71

*So Jesus asked the Twelve, "You do not want to leave too, do you?"*

*Simon Peter answered him, "Lord, to whom will we go? You have the words of eternal life. We have come to believe and know that you are the Holy One of God."*

*Jesus answered them, "Did I not choose you, the Twelve? Yet one of you is a devil!" He meant Judas, son of Simon Iscariot, one of the Twelve, because Judas was going to betray Jesus.*

In the preceding verses, we were told that many of those who had been following Jesus, including that large crowd whom he had fed miraculously, stopped following him. They found his teaching about himself to be too hard for them to accept. They refused to believe it. They rejected Jesus in unbelief.

After these crowds left and stopped following Jesus, he asked his disciples, "You do not want to leave too, do you?" Peter spoke up for the Twelve: "Of course not! You have the words of eternal life. Where else would we go?" An excellent confession of faith, a confession of faith filled with truth. Jesus is the only way to heaven and that way is found only in the Word of God.

To whom shall we go? There are plenty of people in our world today, plenty of places, plenty of radio stations and TV channels, plenty of books and newspapers, and plenty of websites and virtual preachers that all claim to have the truth. All of them claim to have what you need for a better life—either for your life now or the afterlife. But do they have the words of eternal life? Are they the words of Jesus, the Holy One of God? Or are they filled with reason, humanism, and logic? Do they change and twist the meaning of God's Word to simply tell themselves what their itching ears want to hear? Isn't it amazing today how people can read something on the internet or in the newspaper or see it on TV and take it as gospel truth, but when it actually comes to the gospel (what God says in his Word), only questions and speculation and skepticism arise?

Jesus has the words of eternal life. He has given them to us. He has given us the faith to believe them. He has given us eternal life through them. Let's not start looking around for another truth. Let's not start seeing what else is out there. Let's not start buying in to the religion of the world. Let's stick with the truth, the whole truth, and nothing but the truth—the words of Jesus. Better yet, let's get out there and share that truth with others.

*Lord, do not let Satan tempt or mislead me with a good sounding yet deceptive message from a source other than your Word. Amen.*

---

## What Are You Doing?

**John 7:1-5**

*After this, Jesus moved around in Galilee. He did not want to travel in Judea because the Jews were trying to find a way to kill him.*

*Now the Jewish Festival of Shelters was near. So his brothers said to him, "You should leave here and go to Judea so your disciples there can also see the works you are doing. Indeed, no one acts in secret who wants to be known in public. If you are doing these things, show yourself to the world." For even his own brothers did not believe in him.*

The Bread of Life discourse caused many who had been following Jesus to desert him. His popularity was certainly waning. Jesus was not popular with the religious leaders in Jerusalem; they hated him. They hated him enough to want to kill him. What was Jesus' response? Did he chase after those deserting disciples and beg them to come back? Did he rush up to Jerusalem to defend himself and his name in front of the religious leaders? Did he use a show of strength to force others to follow him? Did he launch a huge publicity campaign to win the people over? No. He simply went about his business in Galilee—he went around sharing the good news of God's salvation. He taught the people. He instructed his disciples. He continued to help those in need.

His own brothers said to him, "What are you doing? This isn't getting you anywhere. If you want to be the next big thing, if you want to be popular, you need to leave Galilee, go to Jerusalem, and show yourself to the world." John tells us that Jesus' brothers did not believe in him—not yet anyway. So perhaps this bit of advice, true as it may have been, was said a bit sarcastically; Jesus' brothers were challenging him to do something more if he really thought he was all that. They were making fun of their older brother and his messianic claims.

Jesus would go to the festival when the time was right—he wouldn't allow this sarcastic challenge from his brothers to jeopardize the salvation of the world. He would go to the festival on his own time and in his own way.

Do we ever question Jesus? Do we ever ask him, "What are you doing? Why aren't you helping me? Why are you allowing this or that? Where are you? Don't you know that . . .?" His time. His way. The time would come for Jesus to die. That death would pay for the sins of the world, but the time for that death had not yet come. Jesus has promised us his help, guidance, and protection. He provides it in his way and in his time. He calls us to trust that in all things he is working for our spiritual and eternal good.

*Jesus, I know what you did—you died on the cross to pay for my sins and you rose from the dead to assure me of my salvation. Give me the faith to trust that you know what you are doing in my life. Give me the patience to wait on you and the understanding to see your wisdom. Amen.*

## Timing Is Everything

### John 7:6-9

*So Jesus told them, "The right time for me has not arrived yet, but any time is the right time for you. The world cannot hate you, but it hates me, because I testify about it, that its works are evil. You go up to the festival. I am not going up to this festival yet, because the right time for me has not yet arrived."*

*After he said this, he stayed in Galilee.*

Jesus' brothers had been giving him a hard time. They were trying to tell him how someone who wants to be popular with the people should act. They were telling him that he should go up to Jerusalem to try to win over the people with some more of his miracles—even though they themselves did not yet believe in him as the Son of God.

Jesus knew that everything he did was on a set timetable. Jesus knew that, in time, he would go up to Jerusalem. In time he would go to the festival, but now was not the right time to face a pharisaical hotbed of animosity. The animosity Jesus continually faced was the hatred people had for him because he was honest with them. He was willing to call a spade a spade; he was willing to call sin what it is—evil. Pointing out sinful actions can make people resent and even hate you. But notice why Jesus wanted—why Jesus needed—to point out sin: so that he could lead sinners to repentance, so that he could assure repentant sinners of God's love and forgiveness. Jesus used the law to pave the way for the gospel.

Before we ever take a message of sin and grace, law and gospel, to others, we first must apply that message to ourselves and our own actions, words, and attitudes. Fully aware of our own sin and guilt, and fully assured of our complete forgiveness in Christ, in love we can reach out to others who are caught in sin. The goal is repentance. Rejoice with the angels over that one sinner who does repent, but understand also that, in general, the people of this evil world will hate those who call their actions evil. In the end, though, they are not rejecting us; they are rejecting Jesus.

*Lord, help me always deal with the planks in my own eye; every day lead me to repentance and assure me of my forgiveness in Jesus. Then, and only then, can I ask you to use me to help others caught in sin. Bless your Word that I share with them. Amen.*

## Where Is He?

### John 7:10-13

*However, after his brothers had gone up to the festival, then he also went up, not openly but in a private way.*

*At the festival, the Jews kept looking for him. They asked, "Where is he?" And there was widespread whispering about him in the crowds. Some were saying, "He's a good man." Others were saying, "No, he deceives the people." Yet no one spoke openly about him for fear of the Jews.*

Jesus did go up to the festival—but not because his brothers told him to.

Jesus did go up to the festival—but not to perform miracles to woo the crowd.

Jesus did go up to the festival—but not to become popular with the people.

Jesus went up to the festival because that is where God the Father wanted him to go.

Jesus went up to the festival because he wanted to teach the people God's Word.

Jesus went up to the festival because he was the world's Savior.

People were expecting him. People were looking for him. People were talking about him. People were divided over him. Some liked him; some did not. Some thought he was a good man; some thought he was deceptive. All of them feared the religious leaders because they knew those leaders were out to kill him.

What are we looking for in Jesus: someone who will always do what we ask him? Someone who will woo us with his power? Someone who will make us popular and successful? If that's what we are looking for in Jesus, then just like the people at the festival, we probably won't find it, because in Jesus we have someone who will always do what God the Father wants him to do (not necessarily what we want him to do), which, first and foremost, was to humbly lay down his life as a sacrifice for our sins. In Jesus, we have someone who couples his almighty power and his ability to perform miracles with his wisdom; we have someone who will always do what's best for us—whether we see that as being best or not. In Jesus, we have someone who may not always be popular with those around us, but we have someone who will always love us and be with us no matter what other people say or think about us or him.

*Remind me, Holy Spirit, that I need to look for Jesus no further than in the pages of God's Holy Word. Amen.*

---

## Teaching From God

### John 7:14-19

*When the festival was already half over, Jesus went up to the temple courts and began to teach. The Jews were amazed and asked, "How does this man know what is written without being instructed?"*

*Jesus answered them, "My teaching is not mine, but it comes from him who sent me. If anyone wants to do his will, he will know whether my teaching is from God or if I speak on my own. The one who speaks on his own is seeking his own glory. But he who seeks the glory of the one who sent him—that is the one who is true, and there is no unrighteousness in him. Didn't Moses give you the law? Yet none of you does what the law tells you. Why are you trying to kill me?"*

Jesus did finally go to the festival, he did finally go to the temple courts, and he did finally begin to teach. His teaching impressed the religious leaders—not so much because of what he said or even how he said it but because they knew that Jesus never had any formal training in the Word or as a teacher. As the Son of God, Jesus needed no formal training—either in what to teach or how to teach it. As the Son of God, Jesus not only spoke with authority, but he also spoke the truth. His message of truth was from God the Father. He spoke only what God the Father wanted him to speak.

Since God's Word is the teaching God has given to us and since God's Word is truth and since God's Word tells us why Jesus was killed (so that he could be the sacrifice to pay for our sins), we will do two things: (1) We will, with the faith God has given us, believe this teaching from God. We will trust it; we will not question it; we will not doubt it. And (2) we will, with the joy that comes from believing in Jesus, share this truth with others without twisting or changing the intended meaning or focus.

*Lord Jesus, thank you for teaching me the Word of God in the pages of Scripture. Help me always to believe what you say, and bless me as I share with others what you have taught me. Amen.*

# The Spirit of the Law

**John 7:20-24**

> *"You have a demon!" the crowd answered. "Who is trying to kill you?"*
>
> *Jesus answered them, "I did one work, and you are all amazed. Consider this: Because Moses has given you circumcision (not that it comes from Moses, but from the fathers), you circumcise a man even on the Sabbath. If a man receives circumcision on the Sabbath so that the law of Moses may not be broken, are you angry at me because I made a man completely well on the Sabbath? Stop judging by outward appearance. Instead make a right judgment."*

The crowds of people who had come to Jerusalem for the festival knew little about the plot of the religious leaders to kill Jesus. They thought that Jesus was demon-possessed or a crazy man when he publicly had asked those religious leaders why they were trying to kill him. Jesus wasn't crazy and he wasn't demon-possessed. The religious leaders were plotting his death because they hated him. They hated him because he had healed a man on the Sabbath. "How could he do such a thing!?! How could he break the Sabbath law like that!?!" They hated him because, as they saw it, the people were actually buying in to all of this nonsense. Some were even using the word *Christ* in connection with this man.

Jesus replied by saying, in effect, "If you want to talk about the Sabbath and Sabbath laws, then let's talk about what you do on the Sabbath, when 'no work' is to be done. You can circumcise an eight-day-old baby boy, but I can't heal a man who had been crippled for 38 years? That doesn't make any sense." Not only did that not make sense, but think about this: They were upset with Jesus for healing on the Sabbath, which in their minds meant working on the Sabbath—something contrary to God's law—but these same people were perfectly fine with breaking God's Fifth Commandment as they plotted the death of Jesus.

Their focus on the letter of the law—no work on the Sabbath—had interfered with the spirit of the law—which was to use the Sabbath Day as a day of rest to focus on and worship the Lord. To be sure, God wants us to obey his commandments—and to do so perfectly—but his commandments are summed up in this, "Love the Lord with all your heart, and love your neighbor as yourself" (Luke 10:27). Love is the spirit of the law. May we obey God's law by showing love to those around us.

*Lord, help me to see the big picture of obedience. Help me to see what the right and loving thing to do would be as I use your law as the only guide in my life of faith. Amen.*

---

## Two Reactions

### John 7:25-32

*Some of the people from Jerusalem were saying, "Isn't this the man they want to kill? Yet, look! He's speaking openly, and they don't say a thing to him. Certainly the rulers have not concluded that he is the Christ, have they? But we know where this man is from. When the Christ comes, no one will know where he is from."*

*Then Jesus called out as he was teaching in the temple courts, "Yes, you know me, and you know where I am from. Yet I have not come on my own, but the one who sent me is real. You do not know him. I know him because I am from him, and he sent me."*

*So they tried to arrest him, but no one laid a hand on him, because his time had not yet come.*

*But many in the crowd believed in him and asked, "When the Christ comes, he won't do more miraculous signs than this man, will he?"*

*The Pharisees heard the crowd whispering these things about him, so the chief priests and the Pharisees sent guards to arrest him.*

Jesus continued to teach in the temple courts—and the people continued to talk. "Who is this man? Is he the Christ? Why else would he be here teaching? Who else could do these miracles? But what about the leaders? What do they say? What do they think?"

Jesus addressed the crowd and answered their questions—though in a somewhat veiled sort of way. His answer could be summed up in this way: "You know me because I am the one whom the Father promised to send." This answer was veiled because not everyone knew the one who had sent him—that is, not everyone knew the Father.

The leaders caught what Jesus was implying, and they didn't like it. Some present tried to seize him, though to no avail. They would send the temple guards to arrest Jesus.

There will always be two reactions to Jesus—some will believe in him as their Savior and some will reject him as their Savior. We thank God that he has given us the faith to believe in Jesus as our Savior so that we may receive the salvation he won for all. We thank God for that faith and our salvation by sharing Jesus with others—knowing that not everyone will believe but trusting that at least some will.

*Holy Spirit, empower me to speak your truth in love. Work through my witnessing—better still, work through your Word as you have promised—to gather your elect. Amen.*

# You Cannot Come...Yet

### John 7:33-36

*Then Jesus said, "I am going to be with you only a little while longer. Then I am going away to the one who sent me. You will be looking for me and will not find me, and where I am going to be, you cannot come."*

*Then the Jews said to one another, "Where does this man intend to go that we will not find him? He does not intend to go to the Jews scattered among the Greeks and teach the Greeks, does he? What does he mean by saying, 'You will be looking for me and will not find me, and where I am going to be, you cannot come'?"*

We left Jesus last time as he was about to be arrested by the religious leaders. As they approached him, Jesus talked about going where they couldn't go and about them not being able to find him. Naturally, those sent to arrest him and the crowd who was listening assumed that Jesus was talking about his getaway plan. He was going to flee. He was going to hide. They wouldn't be able to arrest him because they wouldn't be able to find him.

This is not what Jesus was talking about. This was not what he planned to do. The place Jesus would go, first of all, would be the cross. There he would die. There he would suffer the world's punishment for sin. He and he alone could make such a sacrifice—one that would pay for all sin. But Jesus would rise from the dead and ascend into heaven—he would return to the one who had sent him: God the Father. This was a place where this group of people in the temple courtyard, where even his own disciples, could not go—not yet anyway.

Jesus came to the earth physically—as a man. Jesus left the earth physically—as a man. Jesus will return to the earth physically—as a man. The time to go where he has gone has not yet come for any of us. To be sure, all who believe in Jesus will go to be with him where he is, but for you and me, this time has not yet come. This time will come either when our lives here on earth are done and Jesus calls us home or when Jesus returns to earth to take us home to heaven.

*All who believe in you, Lord, will go to heaven. Help me share your Word with others that many more may join us there. Amen.*

---

# Pour Out the Spirit

### John 7:37-39

> *On the last and most important day of the festival, Jesus stood up and called out, "If anyone is thirsty, let him come to me and drink! As the Scripture has said, streams of living water will flow from deep within the person who believes in me." By this he meant the Spirit, whom those who believed in him were going to receive. For the Holy Spirit had not yet come, because Jesus had not yet been glorified.*

Jesus was still at the festival. The religious leaders had sent guards to arrest him as he taught in the temple courts. As we will soon hear, the guards did not arrest Jesus because both they and the crowds were amazed with not only what Jesus taught but also how he was able to teach it.

Jesus returned to a familiar theme and analogy—that of quenching a spiritual thirst with the living water of the gospel. All who believe in Jesus will be filled with the Spirit, and living water will flow from within them—that is, the gospel will continually refresh them with the life-giving message of forgiveness in Jesus, and they will have the spiritual strength to live and share their faith. To be sure, prior to Jesus' ascension and the Day of Pentecost—when the Holy Spirit was poured out in a very special and unique way—the Holy Spirit had already created and worked faith in some of those who were following Jesus. But while there were already believers in Jerusalem, the Holy Spirit had not been given in that special and visible way we associate with Pentecost.

"Thirsty"? Troubled by sin? Bothered by guilt? Troubled by worry? Controlled by fear? Wrestling with stress? "If anyone is thirsty, let him come to me and drink." When we are physically thirsty, we get something to drink. When we are spiritually thirsty, we can drink the life-giving water of the gospel in the Word of God. In Word and sacrament, Jesus will pour out the Holy Spirit to strengthen our faith, assure us of our forgiveness, remind us of his promises, refresh us in our lives of faith, and calm our fears. Dear Christian, drink that water of the gospel regularly and often. Drink it at home. Drink it at church. Offer it to others.

*Holy Spirit, quench my spiritual thirst with the living water of the gospel. Refresh and strengthen me every time I drink it. Move me to drink it often. Amen.*

# Divided

**John 7:40-44**

*After hearing his words, some of the people said, "This is truly the Prophet." Others said, "This is the Christ." But some said, "Surely the Christ does not come from Galilee, does he? Doesn't the Scripture say that the Christ comes from David's descendants and from the little town of Bethlehem where David lived?" So the people were divided because of him. Some of them wanted to arrest him, but no one laid hands on him.*

People today are just as divided over who Jesus is as they were that day in the temple courts.

Who is he?

Many will jump on board and say that he was a prophet, a man with a message of compassion and love.

Many will rally around him and say that he was a good man, a misunderstood man, a man who died for a good cause—or for no reason at all.

Many will look for reasons not to believe in him. Maybe they don't say that the Christ had to come from Bethlehem, not Galilee, or that he had to be from David's family, but they may ask how a man could also be God or how his death could bring salvation.

Many will flat-out deny everything about Jesus—his divinity, his humanity, his miracles, his Word, his teaching, his love, his salvation.

And yet many will still be able to say with the faith God has given them, "He is the Christ." God's Word does not return empty! And there is no other name under heaven given to human beings by which we can be saved! Rejoice that you know that name; rejoice that you know Christ. Rejoice in your salvation by sharing Christ with others.

*Holy Spirit, never let fear of rejection keep me from sharing Christ with others. Amen.*

---

# Not Deceived—He Believed

### John 7:45-53

*Then the guards came to the chief priests and Pharisees, who asked them, "Why didn't you bring him in?"*

*The guards answered, "No one ever spoke the way this man does!"*

*So the Pharisees answered them, "You have not been deceived too, have you? Have any of the rulers or Pharisees believed in him? But this crowd, which does not know the law, is cursed!"*

*One of them, Nicodemus, who had come to Jesus earlier, asked, "Does our law condemn a man before we hear from him and find out what he's doing?"*

*"You are not from Galilee too, are you?" they replied. "Search and you will see that a prophet does not come from Galilee."*

*Then each of them went home.*

The words of Jesus are filled with power. The Word of God is the power of God. The temple guards who had been sent to arrest Jesus had to return to the chief priests and Pharisees without him. "He blew us away. He drew us in. He captivated us. We considered what he told us—it was like nothing we had ever heard." The gospel is like that. The gospel has that effect on people. It can change their hearts.

Sarcastically, scoffing, and incredulous, the religious leaders retorted, "You have not been deceived too, have you?" To paraphrase, "None of us, who have been trained in the law, who truly understand Scripture, have been taken in by this man and his lies. We are too wise for that. We are too strong in our convictions for that to happen. How foolish all these people are! How could they be deceived and led astray so easily?!" Unfortunately, the religious leaders were the ones who had eyes that were ever seeing but never perceiving and ears that were ever hearing but never listening.

Except one—that we know of, anyway. Nicodemus got as close to defending Jesus and confessing his faith in Jesus as his growing faith would allow. He appealed to the law these men claimed to know so well, but they turned on him. They made fun of him; they belittled him. The words of Jesus are filled with power. The gospel can change hearts—look at your own and see how true that is. The Holy Spirit has changed our hearts. We have not been deceived; no, by grace we believe. God grant us the courage to confess that faith.

*Lord, make me bold to confess your name and share your powerful Word. Amen.*

# Who Will Throw the Stone?

### John 7:53–8:7

*Then each of them went home.*

*But Jesus went to the Mount of Olives. Early in the morning, he came back into the temple courts. And all the people kept coming to him. He sat down and taught them.*

*Then the scribes and Pharisees brought a woman caught in adultery and had her stand in the center. "Teacher," they said to him, "this woman was caught in the act of committing adultery. In the Law, Moses commanded us to stone such women. So what do you say?" They asked this to test him, so that they might have evidence to accuse him.*

*Jesus bent down and started writing on the ground with his finger. But when they kept on asking him for an answer, he stood up and said to them, "Let the one among you who is without sin be the first to throw a stone at her."*

The day before, the guards had chosen not to arrest Jesus—they were too intrigued by his teaching. The next day Jesus returned to the temple courts—he again sat down to teach the people. That day brought another, though different, attempt to silence Jesus. If the religious leaders couldn't have Jesus arrested, perhaps they could trap him. They came up with a question that would force Jesus to either break Roman law, which stated that only Rome could execute the death penalty (here, death by stoning), or go against Moses and the Old Testament law, which called for this adulteress to be stoned (never mind the fact that these teachers of the law twisted this death-by-stoning law to fit their needs in this case).

At first, Jesus seemed disinterested, as though he wasn't going to take their bait. They wouldn't let it go. They pressed him for his answer. Jesus gave an answer that is often quoted and repeated to this very day: "Let the one among you who is without sin be the first to throw a stone at her." Jesus turned not just the matter of judging back on the religious leaders, but he also turned the mirror of God's holy law back on them. Jesus was saying, "If you truly want to talk about sin, then perhaps you should start by analyzing and talking about your own sin before you make this woman's sin your business." This reminds us of another often-quoted saying of Jesus about removing the plank from your own eye before worrying about the speck of dust in someone else's.

Each day, God would have us consider our lives in light of the Ten Commandments. Each day, God would have us confess our sins—sins we commit with our eyes, our mouths, and our actions. God would have us confess those sins often and have us turn to Jesus each time for forgiveness. He reminds us that Jesus was punished in our place. He reminds us that he forgives us for Jesus' sake. He empowers us to live a life that reflects the love God has for us.

*Lord, I confess to you that I am a sinner and sin every day in my thoughts, words, and actions, but I ask you to forgive me for Jesus' sake. Assured of your love and forgiveness, empower me to keep your commands and love my neighbor. Amen.*

## Neither Do I Condemn You

### John 8:8-11

*Then he stooped down again and wrote on the
ground.*

*When they heard this, they went away one by one,
beginning with the older men. Jesus was left alone with
the woman in the center. Jesus stood up and said to her,
"Woman, where are they? Has no one condemned you?"*

*"No one, Lord," she answered.*

*Then Jesus said, "Neither do I condemn you. Go, and
from now on do not sin anymore."*

No one was willing to throw the first stone. They all knew
that they were not without sin. Slowly but surely, little by little,
they all went away. Perhaps they went away acknowledging
their own sin. Perhaps Jesus' answer to their question (their
trap) was a call to repentance that God was moving them to
now answer.

When only Jesus and the woman were left, Jesus stood up
and pointed out the obvious—everyone had left; no one had
remained; no one was there to condemn her. But what about
Jesus? Surely the Son of God would condemn her and her sinful
lifestyle—wouldn't he?

No. The Son of God, who had come into the world to seek and
save what was lost and give his life as a ransom for all sinners,
pronounced his forgiveness. "Neither do I condemn you."

To be sure, Jesus was not condoning her sin. He was not
saying it was okay for her to live that way and do those things.
He was not implying that just because she didn't get stoned she
could continue to break the Sixth Commandment. Rather, he
was saying that he forgave her. He was assuring her that he was
willing to be condemned in her place on the cross.

Forgiven sinners look for ways to respond to God's grace. Jesus offered this: "Go, and from now on do not sin anymore." In other words: leave this sinful lifestyle.

God does not condemn us for our sin because he condemned his Son in our place. Jesus was punished in our place. Jesus died in our place. Our sin is paid for. God's forgiveness is ours. What Jesus said to the woman he now says to us: "I do not condemn you. Go, and from now on do not sin anymore."

*Thank you, Jesus! You are my Savior. In you I have forgiveness. In you there is no condemnation. Help me now to live a life that brings you honor and glory. Amen.*

---

# I Am the Light

**John 8:12-14**

*When Jesus spoke to them again, he said, "I am the Light of the World. Whoever follows me will never walk in darkness, but will have the light of life."*

*So the Pharisees said to him, "You testify about yourself. Your testimony is not valid."*

*"Even if I testify about myself," Jesus replied, "my testimony is valid, because I know where I came from and where I am going. But you do not know where I came from or where I am going."*

Isaiah 9:2—"The people walking in darkness have seen a great light."

Isaiah 60:1—"Arise, shine, for your light has come, and the glory of the LORD is dawning upon you."

Jesus knew who he was, and Jesus knew what he was saying. For all who could hear him in the temple courts, Jesus was telling them that he was the promised Messiah. He was telling them that he was the Savior of the world—the Light of the world. Jesus brought light and life to the world—spiritual and eternal life. Jesus brought light and life to us. He healed our spiritual blindness. He shattered through the darkness of our unbelief. He gave us his gift of faith. We see and know him as our Savior. We see and receive the forgiveness we have in him. We see and follow the path of love he would have us walk. Jesus is our light.

Jesus didn't have to prove that to anyone. He didn't have to substantiate his claim with the usual two or three witnesses. He knew what he was saying was the truth. Here Jesus was willing to let his yes be yes. His testimony was valid whether they believed it or not. We thank God that we have believed his testimony. We thank God that we do believe in Jesus. We thank God for the light and life we have through his Son.

*Holy Spirit, help me be a witness to the light. Amen.*

---

# I Am Not Alone

### John 8:15-20

*"You judge according to the flesh. I am not judging anyone. But even if I were to judge, my judgment would be true, because I am not alone, but I am with the Father who sent me. Even in your Law it is written that the testimony of two people is valid. I am one who testifies about myself, and the Father who sent me testifies about me."*

*Then they asked him, "Where is your Father?"*

*"You do not know me or my Father," Jesus answered.*
*"If you knew me, you would also know my Father."*
*He spoke these words while teaching in the temple area*
*near the offering box. But no one arrested him, because*
*his time had not arrived yet.*

Jesus' testimony about himself was valid whether the religious leaders believed it or not. Jesus did not need to prove anything to them. For the sake of his own law, which he himself had written in the Old Testament, Jesus produced his second witness. That witness was God the Father, the one who had sent him into the world. If the religious leaders did not understand or believe the first witness—the Son of God standing in front of them in human flesh—then surely they would not understand or believe the second witness—God the Father whom they could not see or have Jesus run and fetch so they could talk to him. The reality is that they just didn't get it. They didn't believe because they were judging Jesus by human standards—or, more literally they were using their human reason, logic, and flesh to analyze who Jesus was. Flesh only stands in the way of faith.

Jesus has given us ample testimony about himself in his Word. We have the testimony of his miracles. We have the testimony of his teachings. We have the testimony of fulfilled prophecy after fulfilled prophecy. We have the testimony of himself. We have the testimony of the Father. We have the testimony of the Holy Spirit. All this testimony is in the Word. There and there alone the Holy Spirit breaks through and silences our human flesh, our human reason, and our human logic. There and there alone—in the Word of God—the Holy Spirit creates and strengthens our faith in Jesus. We know who he is and where he came from. He came from the Father; he came to be our Savior.

*Thank you, Spirit, for the eyes of faith that see in Jesus my one and only Savior from sin. Amen.*

## But Can I Come?

### John 8:21-24

*So he told them again, "I am going away. You will look for me, and you will die in your sin. Where I am going, you cannot come."*

*So the Jews asked, "He won't kill himself, will he, because he says, 'Where I am going, you cannot come'?"*

*"You are from below," he told them. "I am from above. You are of this world. I am not of this world. That is why I told you that you will die in your sins. For if you do not believe that I am the one, you will die in your sins."*

The religious leaders continued to think from an earthly perspective—trying to use their human reason and logic—to understand Jesus. He said, "I am going away. . . . You cannot come." They thought he was planning to kill himself. Perhaps they thought that would be his way to finally get away from them. Little did they understand that they would kill him on a cross. Even less did they understand that this was God's plan of salvation and Jesus' death would lead to life—his own resurrection, the resurrection of all the dead, and the resurrection to eternal life for all who believe in him.

So, where was Jesus going? He was returning to his Father. He was going to heaven. They could not come—why? They refused to believe in him. As a result, they would die in their sins. They would die eternally in hell for their unbelief. This was not God's will. God our Savior wants all to be saved "and to come to the knowledge of the truth" (1 Timothy 2:4). Notice that God wants salvation for all—he wants all to live—but this salvation and life come only through knowledge, only through faith in Jesus. "Whoever believes and is baptized will be saved, but whoever does not believe will be condemned" (Mark 16:16).

Jesus told these religious leaders that they could not come where he was going. What about us? Can we come? Can we go where Jesus went? Can we go to heaven? Yes! God has given us his gift of faith to know and believe in and trust in Jesus as our only Savior from sin.

*Lord, keep me grounded in your Word that I may never lose my faith or forfeit the salvation you have won for me. Amen.*

---

## Who Are You?

### John 8:25-30

*"Who are you?" they asked.*

*Jesus replied, "What I have been telling you from the beginning. I have many things to say and to judge concerning you. But the one who sent me is true. And what I heard from him, these are the things I am telling the world." They did not understand that he was talking to them about the Father.*

*So Jesus said to them, "When you lift up the Son of Man, then you will know that I am the one, and that I do nothing on my own. But I speak exactly as the Father taught me. The one who sent me is with me. He has not left me alone, because I always do what pleases him."*

*As he was saying these things, many believed in him.*

The Jewish leaders continued to press Jesus, continually asking him, "Who are you?" The more they asked, however, the more they refused to listen to Jesus' answer. The more they asked, the more they refused to believe what he was telling them. The more they asked, the more judgment they brought on themselves as they denied his divinity. The more they asked, the more driven they became to have him crucified.

Let's not let their denial and rejection of Jesus cloud the beautiful answers he had given them regarding his identity—answers that brought many who were listening to faith in him. In these six verses Jesus tells us that he is honest and trustworthy; he is the judge of all; he is the Word made flesh, our Prophet sent by the Father; he is the very Son of God; he is also true man, with human flesh, and as the God-man he would be crucified for the sins of the world; he is sinless and holy, always doing what pleases God the Father; he is the Savior of the world, our substitute in life and death.

*Holy Spirit, bless me with a faith that sees Jesus as my Savior and trusts in him for my salvation. Amen.*

---

## True Freedom

### John 8:31,32

*So Jesus said to the Jews who had believed him, "If you remain in my word, you are really my disciples. You will also know the truth, and the truth will set you free."*

Many people today talk about truth. Many people today talk about freedom, but only the truth of God's Word—only the truth about Jesus—can bring true freedom.

The truth of God's Word is that we are sinners who deserve God's eternal punishment. The truth of God's Word is that, purely out of love, God sent his own Son in human flesh to be our

Savior. The truth of God's Word is that Jesus did not sin; he did not deserve God's eternal punishment, but God punished him anyway in our place. The truth of God's Word is that all who believe in Jesus will live with him in heaven forever.

This truth sets us free. This truth brings true freedom. God has set us free from sin, the devil, and death. Sin no longer condemns us. The devil no longer controls us. And death can no longer hold us.

*Help me, Jesus, to remain in you and your Word so that I never lose the freedom you have won for me. Amen.*

## Children of Abraham

### John 8:33-41

*"We are Abraham's descendants," they answered, "and we have never been slaves of anyone. How can you say, 'You will be set free'?"*

*Jesus answered, "Amen, Amen, I tell you: Everyone who keeps committing sin is a slave to sin. But a slave does not remain in the family forever. A son does remain forever. So if the Son sets you free, you really will be free. I know you are Abraham's descendants. Yet you are looking for a way to kill me, because there is no place for my word in you. I am telling you what I have seen at the side of the Father. As for you, you do what you have heard at the side of your father."*

*"Our father is Abraham!" they answered.*

*"If you were Abraham's children," Jesus told them, "you would do the works of Abraham. But now you are looking*

*for a way to kill me, a man who has told you the truth, which I heard at the side of God. Abraham did not do this. You are doing the works of your father."*

The reason these Jewish religious leaders did not appreciate the freedom they could have had in Christ was because they did not recognize the fact that they were slaves to sin. They claimed Abraham as their father—true enough. They were indeed physical descendants of Abraham, but they certainly didn't act and think like children of Abraham. Abraham was a man who had been willing to entertain and provide a meal for total strangers (strangers who were at his tent to share a message from God with him). The Jewish leaders were ready to kill Jesus simply because he was trying to share a message from God with them. They may have been physical descendants of Abraham, but they were not spiritual descendants of Abraham. They did not believe as Abraham had. They did not live their faith as Abraham had. Rather, they were doing the things that their other father, Satan, would have them do (more on that in the verses that follow). They were slaves. They were not free. They were slaves to sin, not sons of freedom. They were children of the devil, not children of God. The way they spoke, the way they acted, and the things they thought revealed that.

Such was also our state once upon a time. Such was our condition when we were brought into this world. Thankfully, God changed all that. Thankfully, God adopted us into his family through the Sacrament of Baptism. Thankfully, God set us free from sin in Christ. Through faith in Jesus, we are God's children; we are no longer slaves. We are free to live, act, speak, and think as God wants us to.

*Holy Spirit, though I have no physical connection to Abraham, I thank you for making me a spiritual descendant of Abraham. I thank you for blessing me with the same faith, adoption, freedom, and salvation with which you blessed Abraham. Thank you for crediting Christ's righteousness to me by faith. Amen.*

---

## Who's the Liar?

### John 8:41-44

> *"We were not born of sexual immorality!" they said. "We have one Father: God."*
>
> *Jesus replied, "If God were your Father, you would love me, because I came from God and I am here. Indeed, I have not come on my own, but he sent me. Why do you not understand my message? It is because you are not able to listen to my word. You belong to your father, the Devil, and you want to do your father's desires. He was a murderer from the beginning and did not remain standing in the truth, because there is no truth in him. Whenever he lies, he speaks from what is his, because he is a liar and the father of lying."*

Jesus had acknowledged that the Jews to whom he was speaking were physical descendants of Abraham. In that sense Abraham was indeed their father. Yet Jesus had pointed out to them that Abraham was not their spiritual father—they did not believe as Abraham had believed—otherwise they would have believed in Jesus as their Savior. The response of the Jews was to move on from the topic of Father Abraham and claim God as their one and only Father. Certainly, Jesus would have no retort to this!

He did.

Jesus clearly pointed out that God obviously was not their Father. If he were, they would not be rejecting Jesus. If he were, they would not be out to kill him. If he were, they would love him. It was clear to Jesus, the all-knowing Son of God, that neither Abraham nor God was their father. Rather, their father was the devil, Satan himself, the father of lies. Satan was a murderer from the beginning—he murdered the truth, misled Eve, and brought physical and spiritual death into the world. Through his lies he seeks to murder the faith of believers and keep unbelievers in the dark.

Jesus, however, is greater than the father of lies. Jesus is the Way, the Truth, and the Life. In him we have life. From him we have the truth. Through him is the way to eternal life. Thank God that we are spiritual descendants of Abraham and children of the holy God!

*Spirit of Truth, I thank you for bringing me to faith in Jesus. I thank you for making me spiritually alive. I thank you for opening my eyes to the lies of Satan and the truth of God's Word. Help me in my life to defend and share that truth in the world in which I live. Amen.*

## They Believe a Lie

### John 8:45-47

*"But because I tell the truth, you do not believe me. Who of you can convict me of sin? If I am telling the truth, why don't you believe me? Whoever belongs to God listens to what God says. The reason you do not listen is that you do not belong to God."*

People who tell a lie long enough actually start to believe that lie. They no longer remember the truth.

People who are told a lie long enough can actually start to believe that lie and accept it as the truth—even if the evidence around them speaks to the contrary.

These religious leaders had so convinced themselves that the Messiah would be a political leader who would free them from Roman rule that those were the only thoughts they had concerning the Messiah. Because they had been reading the Old Testament in light of a political Messiah for so many years, they could not identify the Messiah for who he was when he was staring them in the face. They believed their own lie. They did not believe God's truth. They did not belong to God. They could not hear what God said.

The lie is out there. Satan is the father of it. The lie is anything suggesting that Jesus is anything less than the Son of God and the Savior of the world. Some promote the lie. Many believe the lie. It is only by God's grace that he has worked in our hearts the faith to believe the truth, the eyes to see Jesus as our Savior, and the ears to hear his Word. The ability to believe, see, and hear had nothing to do with us. By nature we had the same unbelieving hearts, the same blind eyes, and the same deaf ears that these religious leaders had. God is the one who changed that for us. God is the one who changed everything for us. To God be all the credit, praise, and glory, not simply for our salvation but for our ability to know, believe, and trust in Christ alone for that salvation.

*Thank you, God, for claiming me as your own. Because I belong to you, I am able to hear what you say. Amen.*

# With Whom Would Abraham Side?

## John 8:48-59

*The Jews responded, "Are we not right in saying that you are a Samaritan and have a demon?"*

*Jesus answered, "I do not have a demon. On the contrary, I honor my Father, and you dishonor me. I do not seek my own glory. There is one who seeks it, and he is the judge. Amen, Amen, I tell you: If anyone holds on to my word, he will certainly never see death."*

*So the Jews said to him, "Now we know that you have a demon. Abraham died, and so did the prophets. Yet you say, 'If anyone holds on to my word, he will certainly never taste death.' You are not greater than our father, Abraham, are you? He died. And the prophets died. Who do you think you are?"*

*Jesus answered, "If I glorify myself, my glory is nothing. It is my Father who glorifies me, about whom you say, 'He is our God.' Yet you do not really know him, but I do know him. If I said, 'I do not know him,' I would be a liar like you. But I do know him, and I hold on to his word. Your father Abraham was glad that he would see my day. He saw it and rejoiced."*

*The Jews replied, "You aren't even fifty years old, and you have seen Abraham?"*

*Jesus said to them, "Amen, Amen, I tell you: Before Abraham was born, I am." Then they picked up stones to throw at him. But Jesus was hidden and left the temple area.*

Jesus found himself in quite a debate—in quite a disagreement—with the religious leaders of the day. They refused to see or acknowledge him as the eternal Son of God and the promised Savior who was to come. They refused to believe the truth; they insisted on listening to their father—not Abraham, not God, but Satan the father of lies.

They accused Jesus of many things—being a liar, being crazy, being demon-possessed. They did this especially after Jesus made the claim that whoever believes his Word will never see death. These religious leaders went right back to Abraham and cited him as an example of one who died. Their response was "How could Jesus make such a claim?" The claim makes perfect sense if you look at it through the eyes of faith. Jesus is referring to eternal life, not temporal death. "I am the resurrection and the life . . . whoever lives and believes in me will never perish" (John 11:25,26).

The final straw for these religious leaders—which led to looking for stones to kill him—was when Jesus called himself "I am." They did not miss the significance. This was the proper name of God; in Hebrew, Yahweh. Jesus was claiming to be the eternal God who was around not only during the days of Abraham but also before the days of Abraham. Abraham looked forward to Jesus' coming in the flesh. Abraham looked forward to eternal life with Jesus in God's heavenly city. In this debate—which is no debate at all—Abraham would have most definitely sided with Jesus, the eternal Son of God. We can thank God for giving us the faith to believe and do the same! We can thank God that our eyes of faith see Jesus as the eternal Son of God and the promised Savior. We can thank God that our eyes of faith look forward to our heavenly home.

*Lord, may I continue to believe and sing, "I'm but a stranger here! Heaven is my home!" Amen.*

# Why?

### John 9:1-5

> *As Jesus was passing by, he saw a man blind from*
> *birth. His disciples asked him, "Rabbi, who sinned, this*
> *man or his parents, that he was born blind?"*
> *Jesus answered, "It was not that this man sinned, or*
> *his parents, but that God's works might be revealed in*
> *connection with him. I must do the works of him who sent*
> *me while it is day. Night is coming when no one can work.*
> *As long as I am in the world, I am the Light of the World."*

The disciples worded the question slightly different, but they asked the question that is on the minds of people today when something bad happens—"Why?" The disciples wanted to know why this man had been blind from birth. Was it because of his sin or some sin of his parents? They assumed that someone must have done something sinful at some point to anger God and that this was God's way of punishing him. It was a common school of thought. Many people today are no different—we even find ourselves falling into this kind of thinking. When something bad happens in our lives—be it health related, money related, job related, relationship related, or whatever—we are tempted to ask ourselves, "Why me? What did I do? Why is God doing this to me?" Our guilty consciences may even try to answer those questions for us: "It's because you did this. If you hadn't done that, this wouldn't have happened."

Jesus told the disciples that neither the sin of the man nor the sin of his parents caused this blindness. Rather, he said something interesting. He said this happened so that "God's works might be revealed in connection with him." This man was born blind so that some years later, the Son of God veiled in human flesh could show his divine power and help this man in his time of need.

Why? Why me? Why do bad things happen to me? So that God can display his divine power in your life. So that God, as promised, can work all things for your spiritual and eternal good. So that God can give you opportunities to rely on him for help and strength. So that God can give you opportunities to share your faith and your God with others. So that God can help us look forward to the life to come rather than getting too attached to life here on earth.

*Why me, Lord? Why did you choose me? There was nothing good about me that made me desirable to you. I thank you that it was only by grace that you chose me to be your very own. Amen.*

## How Did This Happen?

**John 9:6-12**

*After saying this, Jesus spit on the ground, made some mud with the saliva, and spread the mud on the man's eyes. "Go," Jesus told him, "wash in the pool of Siloam" (which means "Sent"). So he went and washed, and came back seeing.*

*His neighbors and those who had seen him before this as a beggar asked, "Isn't this the one who used to sit and beg?"*

*Some said, "He is the one." Others said, "No, but he looks like him." He kept saying, "I am the one!"*

*So they asked him, "How were your eyes opened?"*

*He answered, "The man who is called Jesus made mud, spread it on my eyes, and told me, 'Go to Siloam and wash.' So I went and washed, and then I could see."*

*"Where is he?" they asked.*
*"I don't know," he said.*

In the previous verses we met this man who had been blind from birth. Thanks to the disciples' "Why?" question, Jesus told us this man had been blind from birth so that the work of God could be displayed in his life. And what a work God displayed! Jesus opened this man's eyes. Jesus very deliberately and very consciously spit on the ground, made some mud with his saliva, and wiped it on the man's eyes. In doing this, there could be no doubt that Jesus was the man who had given this blind man his sight. The man believed. The man trusted. With the faith God had given him, the man went to the Pool of Siloam to wash. With the faith God had given him, the man told others that Jesus was the one who had opened his eyes. He insisted that he was the man they knew who had been blind from birth, the man whom they had seen begging. This miracle and this man brought glory to Jesus and revealed his identity as the Son of God.

Jesus is the same yesterday, today, and forever. The same Jesus who gave this man sight is the same Jesus who can and does display the work of God in our lives. He can heal us and make us better. He can do that through miracles, he can do that through doctors and surgeries, he can do that through nurses and prescriptions—the almighty Son of God can do that; he can do anything. But greater than giving this man physical sight, Jesus had given this man spiritual sight. He gave this man the eyes of faith. Jesus gave us those same eyes of faith, the eyes of faith with which we read this devotion, the eyes of faith which see Jesus not merely as a good and kind man but as the Son of God and our only Savior from sin.

*Lord Jesus, thank you. Thank you for giving me the eyes of faith.*
*Thank you for working in me the faith to know, see, trust, and*

*believe in you as my Savior from sin. As the one who saved me
from hell, help me to trust that you can also use your almighty
power to bring me physical relief and healing as well. Amen.*

## The Response

**John 9:13-17**

*They brought this man who had been blind to the
Pharisees. Now it was a Sabbath day when Jesus made the
mud and opened his eyes. So the Pharisees also asked him
how he received his sight.*

*"He put mud on my eyes," the man told them. "I
washed, and now I see."*

*Then some of the Pharisees said, "This man is not from
God because he does not keep the Sabbath." Others were
saying, "How can a sinful man work such miraculous
signs?"*

*There was division among them, so they said to the
blind man again, "What do you say about him, because
he opened your eyes?"*

*The man replied, "He is a prophet."*

In the rest of John chapter 9 we will see various reactions to
both Jesus and this miracle he performed. We will see division,
resentment, fear, faith, praise, and hate.

In these verses in front of us, on the part of the Pharisees, we
see confusion. How could Jesus be a prophet sent from God if he
did not keep the Sabbath? But whose Sabbath? Jesus may not have
kept their laws, but he did keep the Third Commandment. Jesus
may have done more work on the Sabbath than they allowed,

but he helped a man in need. They were confused as to how an alleged sinner could do something so divine. Their confusion led to division.

In these verses in front of us, on the part of the man whom Jesus had healed, we see faith. He believed that Jesus was sent from God. He believed that Jesus was a prophet. Later in this chapter he will confess and profess that faith even more clearly.

Jesus and his power, sinless life, and compassion need not confuse us. The Holy Spirit has given us the eyes of faith to see Jesus as the one whom God had promised to send—he is the one so full of compassion and power, so free from sin and guilt, that he could save us from sin. His compassion moved him to lay down his life as the payment for our sin. His power enabled him to rise from the dead as a guarantee that our sins are paid for. His sin-free life provides us with the righteousness God demands of us.

*Lead me, Jesus, always to confess you as my Savior and my God. Amen.*

---

# Bullies?

### John 9:18-23

*The Jews still did not believe that he had been blind and received his sight, until they summoned the parents of the man who had received his sight. They asked them, "Is this your son, the one you say was born blind? How is it, then, that he can see now?"*

*"We know that this is our son," his parents answered, "and that he was born blind. But we do not know how he*

*can see now, or who opened his eyes. Ask him. He is old*
*enough. He will speak for himself." His parents said these*
*things because they were afraid of the Jews. For the Jews*
*had already agreed that anyone who confessed that Jesus*
*was the Christ would be put out of the synagogue. That is*
*why his parents said, "He is old enough. Ask him."*

Reactions to Jesus and the miracle he had performed continued. The religious leaders refused to believe that Jesus had
the power or the ability to restore sight. They came up with
possible scenarios. "This isn't the same man. This man wasn't
really blind to begin with. Someone will need to explain this. No
one is going to pull the wool over our eyes." So they brought in
the man's parents and demanded answers. The religious leaders
bullied the man's parents. They intimidated them. It's almost as
if they wanted these parents to lie about their son so that this
miracle—so that Jesus—would just go away. The parents were
afraid. They did not want to be in this position. They were quick
to throw their son under the bus: "We don't know how this
happened. Ask him. He's old enough. Just leave us alone. We
had nothing to do with this." They were afraid.

We pray that our church leaders are never the ones who bully
us about our faith. We pray that if anyone ever puts pressure on
us to deny Jesus or hide our faith, it won't be those who have been
called to feed and nurture our faith with the Word of God. But
bullies will come along. We may bump into them at work, in the
driveway, on a date, or around our own dinner table. Not everyone loves Jesus. Not everyone wants us to live and confess our
faith. Satan certainly doesn't want us to do that. He uses others
to bully us, intimidate us, and make us afraid. He wants us to
deny Jesus—say that Jesus isn't all that important to us, shy away
from defending him and our faith, or simply hide our faith at the
outset of the conversation. Jesus is greater than Satan. Why side

with one who has already been defeated? Why take the side of a loser? Why take the side of someone who talks big—a bully—but cowers in fear before the holy God? God give you the courage to stand firm in your faith and let your light shine brightly.

*Forgive me, Lord, for my fear. Forgive me for the times I have been intimidated by others concerning my faith. Forgive me for failing to put my trust in you. Make me bold to confess you clearly. Amen.*

---

## Back Down?

### John 9:24-34

*So for a second time they summoned the man who had been blind. They told him, "Give glory to God. We know that this man is a sinner."*

*He answered, "I do not know if he is a sinner. One thing I do know: I was blind, and now I see."*

*Then they asked him, "What did he do to you? How did he open your eyes?"*

*He answered, "I already told you, and you did not listen. Why do you want to hear it again? You don't want to become his disciples too, do you?"*

*They ridiculed him and said, "You are his disciple, but we are disciples of Moses. We know that God has spoken to Moses. But this man—we do not know where he comes from."*

*"That's amazing!" the man answered. "You do not know where he comes from, yet he opened my eyes. We know that God does not listen to sinners. But he does listen to anyone who worships God and does his will.*

*From the beginning of time, no one has ever heard of*
*anyone opening the eyes of someone born blind. If this*
*man were not from God, he could do nothing."*
     *They answered him, "You were entirely born in sin-*
*fulness! Yet you presume to teach us?" And they threw*
*him out.*

At this point, perhaps a quick recap of what's going on here
would be helpful. Jesus had healed a man who had been blind
since birth. The disciples had asked the age-old question, "Why?"
Why was this man born blind? Jesus said it would be to his glory.
That's when he performed the miracle; that's when he opened
this man's eyes. Then came the fallout, the reaction—division,
resentment, fear, and hate but also faith and praise.

The religious leaders refused to believe that Jesus was a
prophet, that he had been sent by God, that he was the sinless
Son of God, that he was the promised Savior of the world. They
applied heavy pressure first to the man whom Jesus had healed—
they wanted him to discredit Jesus publicly. Then they applied
even heavier pressure to this man's parents, hoping they would
discredit Jesus. Finally, they brought the man back in and questioned him further—they wouldn't back down. They would do
all they could to discredit Jesus. They put the man under oath.
They made it appear that if this man sided with Jesus, he was
not a believer in the true God. They claimed that no one could
be a disciple of both Moses and Jesus. They badgered him as
they reminded him that Jesus had no credentials—they had no
idea where he had come from; he had no training, no call, no
authority, no clout, no pedigree. They didn't back down—they
ended up throwing him out, excommunicating him.

But the man didn't back down either; in fact, he only grew
stronger. He had an answer for each of their questions or com-
plaints. With each answer he grew more and more bold. He
held on to the truth. He defended Christ. He corrected false

statements. He gave glory to God. He did not back down. God gave him both the faith and the strength to remain true to Jesus. May God do the same for us!

*Lord, in every conversation, let me give glory to you. Make me strong in faith so that I may stand firm and not back down when that faith and my Savior are attacked. Make me strong in my understanding of your Word so that I may always be able to give the reason for the hope that I have. Amen.*

---

# I Can See!

### John 9:35-41

*Jesus heard that they had thrown him out. When he found him, he asked, "Do you believe in the Son of God?"*

*"Who is he, sir," the man replied, "that I may believe in him?"*

*Jesus answered, "You have seen him, and he is the very one who is speaking with you."*

*Then he said, "Lord, I believe!" and he knelt down and worshipped him.*

*Jesus said, "For judgment I came into this world, in order that those who do not see will see, and those who do see will become blind."*

*Some of the Pharisees who were with him heard this and asked, "We are not blind too, are we?"*

*Jesus told them, "If you were blind, you would not hold on to sin. But now that you say, 'We see,' your sin remains."*

The religious leaders were not justified in throwing this man out of their presence or their fellowship; they had no right, no grounds, to excommunicate him. In fact, they should have listened to him and his confession of Christ.

Jesus went to find this man after he had been thrown out. Jesus went to address his fear, his confusion, his questions, and his surprise. Jesus went to strengthen this man's faith, to put this man's eyes of faith into focus. Jesus went to this man so that he would have no doubt that the one who had given him physical sight was the one whom God had promised to send into the world: the Son of Man, the Son of David, the Savior of the world. With 20/20 spiritual vision, the man confessed his faith and worshiped Jesus as his God and Savior.

The Pharisees who witnessed this exchange did not benefit from the same spiritual eye exam. They could only focus on Jesus with their physical eyes. Their physical eyes would never see Jesus as the Son of Man, the Son of David, the Savior of the world. They refused to wear the contacts or glasses of faith; they insisted on remaining spiritually blind. For that, their guilt would remain. If they had seen Jesus as their Savior, in him their guilt would have been removed.

*Holy Spirit, thank you for my eyes of faith. Thank you for my contrite eyes that see and acknowledge my sin and guilt. Thank you for my spiritual eyesight that enables me to see Jesus as my Savior. Thank you for my faith in Jesus that receives both his forgiveness and his righteousness. Amen.*

# I Know My Sheep

### John 10:1-6

*"Amen, Amen, I tell you: Anyone who does not enter the sheep pen by the door, but climbs in by some other way, is a thief and a robber. The one who enters by the door is the shepherd of the sheep. The doorkeeper opens the door for him, and the sheep listen to his voice. He calls his own sheep by name and leads them out. When he has brought out all his own sheep, he walks ahead of them. The sheep follow him because they know his voice. They will never follow a stranger, but will run away from him, because they do not know the voice of strangers." Jesus used this illustration in speaking to the people, but they did not understand what he was telling them.*

We begin a new chapter in the gospel of John—chapter 10, the Good Shepherd chapter of the Bible. In the first six verses of this chapter, Jesus painted the picture of a typical open-air sheep pen. The walls of the sheep pen were built either out of rock or timber—the material is immaterial. The point is that there was only one entrance into the sheep pen. There was only one gate, and that gate was tended by the watchman. The watchman had strict instructions to allow only the shepherd of the sheep inside the pen to enter through the gate and lead out the sheep. If someone else entered the pen, he did not enter through the gate. If someone else entered the pen, he was a thief or robber.

The sheep, though not intelligent animals, would follow only the voice of their shepherd. Similarly, the shepherd knew his sheep. He knew them by name. He knew if one was missing. He knew when to lead them out of the pen and when to bring them back into the pen. He knew where to lead them. He knew how to lead them. He knew his sheep and his sheep knew him.

Jesus will state it himself later in the chapter, but he is our Shepherd. He is the Good Shepherd. Jesus protects us. Jesus wants no one and no thing to steal us from him. As the walls around the pen guarded and protected the sheep from wild animals and thieves, so Jesus guards and protects us from false teaching and false prophets who want to steal us away from him. Just as the shepherd led his sheep out to pasture and streams of water, Jesus leads us; he feeds us with Word and sacrament. He guides us through life. Our Good Shepherd is the one who has given us the faith to hear, know, and follow his voice.

*Guard and protect me, Lord, from all harm and danger—spiritual harm and physical danger. Strengthen me and my faith through Word and sacrament. Guard and protect me from all lies that threaten my relationship with you. Amen.*

## I Am the Door

**John 10:7-10**

*So Jesus said again, "Amen, Amen, I tell you: I am the door for the sheep. All who came before me were thieves and robbers, but the sheep did not listen to them. I am the door. Whoever enters through me will be saved. He will come in and go out, and find pasture.*

*"A thief comes only to steal and kill and destroy. I came that they may have life and have it abundantly."*

In the previous verses we heard Jesus say that he was the Shepherd of the sheep. He spoke about a watchman standing at the gate of the walled-in sheep pen—a sheep pen with only one entrance—who would allow only the sheep's shepherd into the pen. In the verses of the next devotion we will hear Jesus say, "I am the Good Shepherd." In those verses we will consider what sets Jesus apart from all other shepherds.

In these verses Jesus continued with the shepherd-sheep metaphor but from a slightly different angle. Jesus said, "I am the door." No more watchman standing at the door granting permission to the shepherd to come in and go out. No more wooden door for the watchman to open and close for the shepherd and his sheep. No, here Jesus said, "I am the door."

Picture the same sheep pen you did in our last devotion—an open-air pen with a rock wall all the way around it except for one opening at one end of the pen. This pen was typical of sheep pens in or near town. It would have included a wooden door and a watchman at the one opening in the rock wall. The sheep pen Jesus spoke of in these verses would have been typical of the pens out in the fields. These pens would have been built the same way—only they would have had no wooden door and no watchman. Rather, the shepherd would be the door. The shepherd would lie down in that opening at night, and he would determine who could come in and go out.

Jesus is the door. The only way to heaven is through him. He is the Way, the Truth, and the Life. Until he brings us safely home to heaven, we "go out" and "come in" through him. He is the one who guards and protects us spiritually; he guards and protects our faith from false prophets and false teachings, the robbers and thieves. He is the one who leads us out to nourish our faith—he feeds our faith with Word and sacrament. He is the only way in and the only way out. In him alone are we saved. By him alone is our faith protected and nourished.

*Thank you, Jesus, for being my door. Thank you for being my one and only way to heaven—you alone are the sure way to heaven. Thank you, Jesus, for protecting me and my faith from false teaching and nourishing my faith with the truth of the gospel. Amen.*

## I Am the Good Shepherd

### John 10:11-18

*"I am the Good Shepherd. The Good Shepherd lays down his life for the sheep. The hired man, who is not a shepherd, does not own the sheep. He sees the wolf coming, leaves the sheep, and runs away. Then the wolf attacks the sheep and scatters them. Because he works for money, he does not care about the sheep.*

*"I am the Good Shepherd. I know my sheep and my sheep know me (just as the Father knows me and I know the Father). And I lay down my life for the sheep. I also have other sheep that are not of this sheep pen. I must bring them also, and they will listen to my voice. Then there will be one flock and one shepherd. This is why the Father loves me, because I lay down my life so that I may take it up again. No one takes it from me, but I lay it down on my own. I have the authority to lay it down, and I have the authority to take it up again. This is the commission I received from my Father."*

What sets Jesus apart as the Good Shepherd? He was willing to die (he did die) for his sheep. He was not going to abandon us (he did not abandon us) when certain death (eternal death) threatened us. Instead, he stepped between us and death. He stepped between us and God's just anger. He stepped between us and God's wrath and punishment for our sins. He laid down his life. He suffered and died on the cross. He paid for our sins. He earned our forgiveness.

What sets Jesus apart as the Good Shepherd? He is alive, our living Shepherd. Jesus laid down his life only to take it up again. He laid it down willingly; he took it up victoriously. In Jesus we have a living Shepherd who not only spared us eternal punishment and saved us from sin but who now lives to lead and guide, guard and protect, and feed and nourish us. He truly is the Good Shepherd—our Good Shepherd.

*I praise you, Jesus, for your love and dedication. I thank you for not abandoning me. I thank you for laying down your life to pay for my sins. I praise you for your resurrection from the dead that assures me that I too shall live. Empower me always to put my trust in you, my living Shepherd. Amen.*

## Still Divided

### John 10:19-21

*There was a division among the Jews again because of these words. Many of them were saying, "He has a demon and is out of his mind! Why listen to him?" Others said, "These are not the sayings of someone demon-possessed. Can a demon open the eyes of the blind?"*

Perhaps we find it hard to understand how someone, after listening to Jesus talk about being the Good Shepherd, could still refuse to believe in him. Some of the people who had heard Jesus talk about laying down his life for them scoffed. They shrugged it all off; they shrugged off Jesus. They claimed that he was demon-possessed and madly insane. Perhaps we find it hard to understand how someone today, after reading these words of Jesus in John chapter 10, after hearing about a Good Shepherd who leads and guides, guards and protects, and feeds and nourishes his sheep, still refuses to believe in him. But that's just how stubborn an unbelieving heart can be.

More than that, that's just how stubborn our unbelieving hearts had been. The faith we have in Jesus, the trust we place in him as our Good Shepherd, is nothing we did; it's nothing we decided to have or do; it's nothing we even wanted. We are no different than the Jews who rejected Jesus back then or the people who reject him today, but the Holy Spirit changed everything for us. The Holy Spirit gave us the gift of faith. The Holy Spirit opened our eyes and our hearts to see and believe in Jesus as our Good Shepherd who laid down his life for our sins only to take that life up again. While people are still divided over Jesus today, we can thank God that we are on the side of those who believe in him, and we can be confident that if the Holy Spirit can bring people like us to faith in Jesus, then he can bring anyone to faith in Jesus.

*People will always be divided over you, Jesus, but I pray that more and more people would be brought to faith in you. I pray that more and more of your sheep would share their faith so that more and more of your other sheep may be brought into your sheep pen. Amen.*

# The Question Is Answered

## John 10:22-30

*Then the Festival of Dedication took place in Jerusalem. It was winter, and Jesus was walking in the temple area in Solomon's Colonnade.*

*So the Jews gathered around Jesus, asking, "How long will you keep us in suspense? If you are the Christ, tell us plainly."*

*Jesus answered them, "I did tell you, but you do not believe. The works I am doing in my Father's name testify about me. But you do not believe, because you are not my sheep, as I said to you. My sheep hear my voice. I know them, and they follow me. I give them eternal life, and they will never perish. No one will snatch them out of my hand. My Father, who has given them to me, is greater than all. No one can snatch them out of my Father's hand. I and the Father are one."*

Roughly two months had passed since Jesus spoke about being the Good Shepherd. He was now in Jerusalem celebrating the Festival of Dedication, or Hanukkah, also called the Festival of Lights. The Jews surrounded him and demanded to know if he truly was the Christ. If only they had honestly wanted to know the answer! They didn't. They refused to believe that Jesus was the Christ. How do we know? Jesus already had answered that question for them—several times, in many different ways: his "I am" statements, his miracles, his teaching, his life, his Father's voice from the cloud at his Baptism. In these verses he plainly said, "I and the Father are one." Jesus claimed that he is God. He is God, but they hadn't believed Jesus before this and they weren't about to believe him now—they were not his sheep.

But did you notice what Jesus said about his sheep? About us? About you? About me? "No one can snatch them out of my Father's hand." No matter what happens to us in this life, no matter what threatens us—be it physical or spiritual, be it friend or foe—no one and no thing can snatch us out of our Savior's or our heavenly Father's hand. False teachers and their false teachings won't, health and medical issues won't, our own sin and doubt won't, angels and demons won't—nothing in all creation will. Nothing will ever separate us from the love of God in Christ Jesus our Lord; nothing will snatch us out of his hand—not even death. In fact, death will simply take us from this life of sorrow home to heaven where we will be with Jesus forever.

*May these words always be a source of comfort and hope for me, Lord, no matter what happens to me or my loved ones in this life. Amen.*

## Has Anything Changed

**John 10:31-39**

*Again the Jews picked up stones to stone him. Jesus answered them, "I have shown you many good works from my Father. For which of these are you going to stone me?"*

*"We are not going to stone you for a good work," the Jews answered, "but for blasphemy, because although you are a man, you make yourself out to be God."*

*Jesus answered them, "Is it not written in your Law, 'I said you are gods'? If he called those people 'gods,' to whom the word of God came, and the Scripture cannot*

*be broken, what about the one whom the Father set
apart and sent into the world? Do you accuse me of
blasphemy because I said, 'I am God's Son'? If I am not
doing the works of my Father, do not believe me. But if
I am doing them, even if you do not believe me, believe
the works so that you will know and understand that the
Father is in me, and I am in the Father."*

 *So they tried to arrest him again, but he eluded
their grasp.*

It's interesting to note that if you were to talk to religious skeptics today about Jesus, if you were to talk with agnostics or atheists today about Jesus, many of them would say that Jesus never claimed to be God. They would say that he was a good man, a kind man, and a wise teacher, but God?—No. He never claimed to be God.

The religious leaders two thousand years ago would disagree. They listened to Jesus. They heard what he said, and they got the point. They knew exactly what Jesus was saying. Jesus was claiming equality with God the Father; he was claiming that he was of one being with the Father; he was claiming that he was God. The religious leaders were ready to stone him for blasphemy—the only problem is that claims like those from the mouth of Jesus are not blasphemous.

Has anything changed? Not really. People then and people today refuse to believe that Jesus is more than just a man. They deny all evidence. They suppress all claims. They get lost in all arguments. They build their case on reason, logic, and lies. They come up with their answer before they know the question. They oppose Jesus and all who follow him. They belittle Jesus and condescend those who follow him.

Has anything changed? Jesus is the same yesterday, today, and forever. Jesus is still true God and true man in one person.

Jesus still sends his Holy Spirit to break through the darkness of unbelief with the light of the gospel to bring people to faith in him. That's our Jesus. That's our God. That's our Savior.

*Jesus, use me and your Word and all who preach it to change the hearts of those who still oppose you. Amen.*

---

## Encouraging

### John 10:40-42

*He went back across the Jordan to the place where John had been baptizing earlier, and he stayed there.*
*Many came to him and were saying, "John never did a miraculous sign, but everything John said about this man was true." And many believed in him there.*

We have seen and heard the religious leaders of Jesus' day question him, put him on the spot, oppose him, and ridicule him; they tried to undermine him and his authority and his message; they even tried to kill him twice. They certainly did not believe in him.

Opposition. Unbelief.

Lest we forget, lest we become discouraged, lest we think that everyone hates and opposes Jesus, John saw fit—the Holy Spirit saw fit—to include some good news, some encouraging news. He takes us to a place where John the Baptist had preached and baptized. He takes us to a place where John pointed to Jesus as the Lamb of God who takes away the sin of the world. Jesus went to that place across the Jordan River. He taught the people. The people believed. God's Word had brought them to faith. Faithful preaching and teaching had brought them to faith. Many people believed in Jesus.

We may not always see success when we share the gospel. Not everyone will believe or even care when we share our faith with them, but John gives us this encouragement today: "Many believed in [Jesus] there." God's Word works. He will use it to bring people to faith in Jesus. God bless your sharing of his Word!

*Holy Spirit, overcome my doubt and my fear, overcome any feelings of discouragement as I share your Word with others. Help me put my confidence not in myself and my words but in you and your Word. Amen.*

---

## What's He Up To?

### John 11:1-6

*Now a certain man named Lazarus was sick. He was from Bethany, the village of Mary and her sister Martha. This Mary, whose brother Lazarus was sick, was the same Mary who anointed the Lord with perfume and wiped his feet with her hair.*

*So the sisters sent a message to Jesus, saying, "Lord, the one you love is sick!"*

*When Jesus heard it, he said, "This sickness is not going to result in death, but it is for the glory of God, so that the Son of God may be glorified through it."*

*Jesus loved Martha and her sister and Lazarus. Yet when he heard that Lazarus was sick, he stayed in the place where he was two more days.*

Today we begin a familiar and much-loved chapter of the Bible. We've heard Jesus' Bread of Life discourse (John chapter 6). We've rejoiced in our Good Shepherd (John chapter 10). Chapter 11 of John's gospel will give us the comforting words of our living Savior, "I am the resurrection and the life. Whoever believes in me will live, even if he dies. And whoever lives and believes in me will never perish."

Interesting, then, that sickness sets the stage for the events and lessons and comfort that will soon unfold. Already in these first six verses of the chapter, we can tell that Jesus was up to something. He had a plan. All of it would be for God's glory. All of it would show that whoever believes in Jesus will have life.

No parentheses but perhaps a parenthetical thought. God has a plan for each one of us. That doesn't mean bad things won't happen to us. That doesn't mean God doesn't love us. Lest we forget, we live in a sin-filled world. We live in a world where Satan roams. Bad things happen in this sin-filled, Satan-roamed world, but the God of grace can use these bad things for our spiritual and eternal good. We are reminded that we have somewhere to turn and someone to whom to turn when bad things happen. We are reminded that God invites us to call upon him in the day of trouble. We are reminded that the God who was powerful enough to create the world can do anything and also that the God who was wise enough to create the world will do only what's best.

How will Jesus demonstrate his power and wisdom in the lives of his good friends Mary and Martha and in the life of their brother who was sick? What's Jesus up to? We'll have to wait and see, but for now, know that it is for the good of those who love him.

*Forgive me, Lord, for blaming you when bad things happen to me. Help me to see your hand working good through all the bad. And even if I never see the good your hand works, help me to trust that you're doing what's best for me and my relationship with Jesus. Amen.*

## Let Us Also Go

### John 11:7-16

*Then afterwards he said to his disciples, "Let's go back to Judea."*

*The disciples said to him, "Rabbi, recently the Jews were trying to stone you. And you are going back there again?"*

*Jesus answered, "Are there not twelve hours of daylight? If anyone walks around during the day, he does not stumble because he sees this world's light. But if anyone walks around at night, he stumbles because there is no light on him."*

*He said this and then told them, "Our friend Lazarus has fallen asleep, but I am going there to wake him up."*

*Then the disciples said, "Lord, if he has fallen asleep, he will get well."*

*Jesus had been speaking about his death, but they thought he was merely talking about ordinary sleep. So Jesus told them plainly, "Lazarus is dead. And I am glad for your sake that I was not there, so that you may believe. But let us go to him."*

*Then Thomas (called the Twin) said to his fellow disciples, "Let's go too, so that we may die with him."*

Last we heard, Jesus' good friend Lazarus was sick—very sick, deathly sick—but Jesus didn't rush to Bethany. He didn't rush to the aid of his friend. He waited around. For a couple of days he waited around. We ask ourselves, "What's Jesus up to?" He told us. He told us that this would be to his Father's glory. He had a plan. He had a plan to demonstrate his power over death as the Son of God. He planned to give us a preview of his own resurrection from the dead. So he waited and, as he waited, Lazarus died—just as Jesus knew he would. Now after Lazarus' death, Jesus told his disciples it was time to go to Judea—to Bethany.

The disciples quickly reminded Jesus that the last time he was in Judea, the Jews tried to kill him. Jesus knew this. Jesus knew this would ultimately be God's plan for him. He knew the Jews wanted to kill him. He knew that when he raised Lazarus from the dead, the Jews would want to kill him all the more. But the thought of his own death did not keep him from going to Judea—rather, the thought of his own death was what took him to Judea. Jesus was advancing God's plan of salvation another step closer to the cross—and his own empty tomb.

As for Thomas and his comment, "Let's go too, so that we may die with him," is that a statement of faith and commitment to Jesus—"If Jesus is going to go and if he is going to die, then count me in; I'm going with him; I'm going to support him even if it means losing my life"? Or is it a pessimistic reaction that throws in the towel—"Here's the end; let's get this over with"? We can't say for sure. Regardless, Thomas and the other disciples sensed that the end was near. But they would have to wait to see how Jesus' death brings life to all. We today, who know that Jesus' death was followed by his resurrection, are blessed to see God's completed salvation plan for us. May God give us the faith, courage, and commitment to follow the one who lived, died, and rose in our place regardless of the cost.

*Living Savior, help me to follow wherever you may lead me. Give me understanding and courage as I live my life of faith. Amen.*

## Resurrection and Life

### John 11:17-27

*When Jesus arrived, he found that Lazarus had already been in the tomb for four days.*

*Bethany was near Jerusalem, about two miles away. Many Jews had come to Martha and Mary to comfort them concerning their brother.*

*When Martha heard that Jesus was coming, she went to meet him, while Mary was sitting in the house.*

*Martha said to Jesus, "Lord, if you had been here, my brother would not have died. But even now I know that whatever you ask from God, God will give you."*

*Jesus said to her, "Your brother will rise again." Martha replied, "I know that he will rise in the resurrection on the Last Day." Jesus said to her, "I am the resurrection and the life. Whoever believes in me will live, even if he dies. And whoever lives and believes in me will never perish. Do you believe this?"*

*"Yes, Lord," she told him. "I believe that you are the Christ, the Son of God, who was to come into the world."*

Jesus arrived in Bethany, and Lazarus was dead. Plenty of people had come to comfort Mary and Martha, but when Martha heard that Jesus was coming, she went out to meet him.

Jesus knew what he was about to do. Martha did not, but she did trust and believe that with Jesus anything was possible. She knew that Jesus could have kept Lazarus from dying; she knew also—and she confessed—that God would give Jesus "whatever" he asked. Would he ask God to bring Lazarus back to life? The implication is there, but when Jesus told Martha that her brother would rise again, she jumped immediately to the resurrection on the Last Day as she confessed her faith and her belief in the life after this one. Jesus strengthened that faith with the declaration that he was indeed the resurrection and the life; he promised—he guaranteed—that whoever believes in him will never die.

Jesus has chosen not to use his almighty power to keep our loved ones from dying or bring them back from the dead after they have died. He has promised us something far greater! He has promised that our loved ones who die believing in him will enter eternal life immediately—they will live forever in heaven and never die. Let's not forget the greater miracle as the stage is set for Jesus to bring Lazarus out of the tomb! The greater miracle is that sinners like you and I will live forever in heaven with the holy God because of Jesus!

*Lord, thank you for the faith to confess you as the Christ, the Son of the living God. Thank you for your promise of eternal life. Until you make that promise a reality for me in heaven, comfort me and all who mourn the loss of a loved one with the assurance that whoever believes in you will never die. Amen.*

## Jesus Wept?

**John 11:28-37**

*After she said this, Martha went back to call her sister Mary. She whispered, "The Teacher is here and is calling for you."*

*When Mary heard this, she got up quickly and went to him. Now Jesus had not yet gone into the village, but was still where Martha met him. The Jews who were with Mary in the house consoling her saw that she got up quickly and left. So they followed her, supposing she was going to the*

*tomb to weep there. When Mary came to where Jesus was*
*and saw him, she fell at his feet and said, "Lord, if you had*
*been here, my brother would not have died."*

*When Jesus saw her weeping, and the Jews who came*
*with her also weeping, he was deeply moved in his spirit*
*and troubled.*

*He asked, "Where have you laid him?"*

*They told him, "Lord, come and see."*

*Jesus wept.*

*Then the Jews said, "See how he loved him!" But some*
*of them said, "Could not he who opened the eyes of the*
*blind man have kept this man from dying?"*

The shortest verse in the Bible is only two words long—"Jesus wept." And yet this shortest verse of the Bible is filled with love and emotion; it is filled with the humanity of Jesus; it is filled with an unselfish concern that is credited to us by faith; it is filled with a sadness at just how polar opposite death is to what God had intended at creation; it is filled with sympathy for those who were hurt by this loss. The list could go on. The fact is, Jesus wept.

His tears, however, were a far cry from the uncontrolled wailing and carrying on that were common in that culture at the death of a friend or relative. His tears were a far cry from the selfish tears people shed when their thoughts at the death of a loved one are more on themselves and how their lives will be different now and how much they will miss this person than on the believer who died and is now in heaven. Jesus' tears were a far cry from the ignorant or naïve tears of those who do not understand that, for believers, death means life.

Jesus' tears were not for himself; he did not shed them because he missed Lazarus—Jesus had in mind what he was about to do even before Lazarus had died. That's why he waited around, why he delayed going to Bethany. Jesus was sad for his friends; their mourning moved him. Jesus was sad that death was in the world because of sin. In his emotion, in his empathy, and in his sympathy we see his humanity; we see his unselfish love; we see our substitute in life. Everything good and sinless that Jesus did in life is credited to us by faith. In him we are holy and righteous.

*Already holy and righteous before you through faith in Jesus, Lord, help my first thought in life always to be for those around me rather than for myself. Amen.*

# To God Be the Glory

### John 11:38-44

*Jesus was deeply moved again as he came to the tomb. It was a cave, and a stone was lying against it. "Take away the stone," he said.*

*Martha, the dead man's sister, told him, "Lord, by this time there will be an odor, because it has been four days."*

*Jesus said to her, "Did I not tell you that if you believe, you will see the glory of God?" So they took away the stone.*

*Jesus looked up and said, "Father, I thank you that you heard me. I knew that you always hear me, but I said this for the benefit of the crowd standing here, so that they may believe that you sent me." After he said this, he shouted with a loud voice, "Lazarus, come out!"*

*The man who had died came out with his feet and his hands bound with strips of linen and his face wrapped with a cloth. Jesus told them, "Loose him and let him go."*

Jesus finally made his way to the tomb—*finally* because when he first heard that Lazarus was sick, he intentionally waited for Lazarus to die. At that time he had told the messenger and his disciples that this would all be to the glory of God. *Finally* also because even after Jesus had arrived at Bethany, he didn't rush right to the tomb. He spoke first with Martha, then with Mary. He offered both of them the comfort that only the Lord of life could offer. Finally, he went to the tomb.

He asked that the stone be rolled away. Martha protested. Martha pointed out the obvious—"But, Lord, he stinks! He's been dead for four days." Jesus redirected Martha to his previous comments about the resurrection and the life, the words he had given the messenger: Lazarus' sickness would be to the glory of God. He would live. Jesus also redirected the thoughts and hearts of the people away from death and the tomb heavenward to the source of life and God the Father. Jesus was pointing the people who would witness this miracle to God the Father who had heard the prayer of his Son. Jesus was directing the people to give glory to God the Father.

Jesus, the Resurrection and the Life, gave the people a preview of his own resurrection from the dead. Death would not hold him. Death would have no power over him. With his own resurrection he defeated death and won the victory; he gave his victory over death to you and me. Death holds no power over us. We shall not die but live. Because he lives, we also shall live. By raising Lazarus from the dead, Jesus has given us a preview of our own resurrection from the dead on the Last Day when we will live with him for all eternity. To God be the glory!

*Lord Jesus, in all I do, in all I say, as I use the gifts you have given me, help me—remind me—to direct all glory to God the Father. Amen.*

# One for All

### John 11:45-53

*Therefore many of the Jews who came to Mary and saw what Jesus did believed in him. But some of them went to the Pharisees and told them what Jesus had done. So the chief priests and the Pharisees called a meeting of the Sanhedrin. They asked, "What are we going to do, because this man is doing many miraculous signs? If we let him go on like this, everyone will believe in him. Then the Romans will come and take away both our place and our nation."*

*But one of them, Caiaphas, who was high priest that year, said to them, "You know nothing at all. You do not even consider that it is better for us that one man die for the people than that the whole nation perish." He did not say this on his own, but, as high priest that year, he prophesied that Jesus was going to die for the nation, and not only for that nation, but also in order to gather into one the scattered children of God.*

*So from that day on they plotted to kill him.*

The fact that Jesus raised Lazarus from the dead had an impact on the people who saw it or heard about it. Some of them, as John said, put their faith in Jesus. Others weren't sure what to make of it—they were confused. And the religious leaders hated Jesus all the more. Their hate for Jesus was driven by jealousy—they didn't want Jesus becoming so popular that the people stopped following them. Their hate for Jesus was driven by fear—they didn't want the Romans stepping in and taking away all of their authority simply because they couldn't contain some prophet. Their hate for Jesus was driven by selfishness—they didn't want to lose their "place" (whether that was the temple itself, their homes in Jerusalem, or simply their place on the Jewish high court).

The high priest stood up to take control of the situation. He basically said, "We're not going to let any of that happen! We're going to get rid of Jesus. It is better that one man die than all of us. It's better that one Jew die than to have the Romans make life miserable for every Jew." He was speaking politically. He was speaking about a human solution to a sticky problem. Without realizing it, however, he spoke prophetically. God used him to proclaim his divine solution to people's sin. One man would die for all. That one man was his own Son, the God-man, Jesus Christ. In their plot to kill Jesus, they led Jesus to the cross and the very place where he would pay for the sins of the whole world. One man's death would pay for all people's sin. One for all.

*Such a simple plan! Such a generous plan! Such a loving plan! Such a sacrificial plan! Such a selfless plan! Jesus, I thank you for taking not only my place under the hand of God's eternal punishment but the place of every human being. I thank you for your death that paid for my sins—not only for mine but for the sins of the whole world. Amen.*

## Not Yet

### John 11:54-57

*Therefore Jesus no longer walked about openly among the Jews. Instead he withdrew into a region near the wilderness, to a town called Ephraim. And he stayed there with his disciples.*

*The Jewish Passover was near, and many went up to Jerusalem from the country to purify themselves before the Passover. They kept looking for Jesus and asking one another as they stood in the temple area, "What do you think? He certainly won't come to the Festival, will he?" The chief priests and the Pharisees had given orders that if anyone knew where Jesus was, he should report it so that they could arrest Jesus.*

When Jesus raised Lazarus from the dead, it caused quite a stir. Many people believed. As we might imagine, though, this miracle really got under the skin of the chief priests and Pharisees. They wanted all the more to get rid of Jesus. They put out the word that anyone who saw Jesus out in public should report it—they wanted to arrest him, or worse.

Jesus knew that he had come into the world in human flesh to die, but he also knew that his time to die had not yet come—it was not time for his crucifixion. So he withdrew, he no longer moved about publicly and went to the desert region near Ephraim, not because he was afraid or no longer willing to die but because he knew and was willing to submit to his heavenly Father's timetable, his heavenly Father's plan of salvation.

What an amazing Savior we have! Willing to die for us! Willing to take our punishment upon himself! Willing to do whatever was necessary—willing to do all that was necessary to save us but not until the time was right. Jesus was obedient to his Father's timetable. Jesus fully submitted to his Father's plan of salvation. And because he did, we have eternal life. Amazing!

*Lord Jesus, you did it. You saved me from sin. You did what needed to be done, because I couldn't. You did it when it needed to be done, because God the Father demanded it. Thank you. Amen.*

## Poured-Out Love

### John 12:1-11

*Six days before the Passover, Jesus came to Bethany, the hometown of Lazarus, who had died, the one Jesus raised from the dead. They gave a dinner for him there. Martha was serving, and Lazarus was one of those reclining at the table with him.*

*Then Mary took about twelve ounces of very expensive perfume (pure nard) and anointed Jesus' feet and wiped his feet with her hair. The house was filled with the fragrance of the perfume.*

*But one of his disciples, Judas Iscariot, who was going to betray him, said, "Why wasn't this perfume sold for three hundred denarii and given to the poor?" He did not say this because he cared for the poor, but because he was a thief. He held the money box and used to steal what was put into it.*

*Jesus replied, "Leave her alone. She intended to keep this for the day of my burial. Indeed, the poor you always have with you, but you are not always going to have me."*

*A large crowd of the Jews learned that he was there. They came not only because of Jesus, but also to see Lazarus, whom he raised from the dead. So the chief priests made plans to kill Lazarus too, because it was on account of him that many of the Jews were leaving them and believing in Jesus.*

Mary loved Jesus—she was a devoted, faithful follower; Jesus was her Lord and Savior. She poured out that love for Jesus— literally. She poured a generous amount of expensive perfume on his feet and then humbly wiped his feet with her hair. Loving. Devoted. Faithful. Generous. Humble. Her faith in Jesus was obvious. Jesus made it clear that her faith and devotion were not misplaced. Jesus informed the group that this had been done in anticipation of his burial—whether Mary had realized that or not.

Judas, of course, was upset. When he saw Mary pour out that expensive perfume on Jesus' feet, he saw money being poured down the drain. His concern was not for the poor but for himself. He knew that the more money they had coming into their little treasury, the more money he would have coming into his own little nest egg. Judas loved himself. Judas was devoted to himself. Judas was faithful to his own plans. Judas was generous when it came to his own needs. Judas showed a false humility in his hypocritical concern for the poor.

Jesus poured out his love for us on the cross as he shed his blood to pay for our sins. Talk about love. Talk about devotion. Talk about faithfulness. Talk about generosity. Talk about humbleness. In him our sins are covered. In him we have forgiveness for own selfish ambitions and desires. By him we are empowered to show him our love as we show love to others. Loving, devoted, faithful, generous, humble—in Christ that's what we are; in Christ that's what we'll be.

*Forgive me, Jesus, for having the same self-centered sinful nature as Judas. Forgive me, Jesus, for listening to the old Adam. Assure me of your love and forgiveness. Help me to pour out my love for you by pouring out that love on others. Amen.*

# Hosanna!

### John 12:12-16

*The next day, the large crowd that had come for the Festival heard that Jesus was on his way to Jerusalem. Taking palm branches, they went out to meet him, shouting, "Hosanna! Blessed is he who comes in the name of the Lord—the King of Israel!"*

*Jesus found a young donkey and sat on it, just as it is written: "Do not be afraid, daughter of Zion. Look! Your King is coming, seated on a donkey's colt."*

*At first, his disciples did not understand these things. But when Jesus was glorified, then they remembered that these things had been written about him and that they did these things for him.*

The last week of Jesus' life on earth began as Jesus arrived in Jerusalem on Palm Sunday. In fulfillment of Zechariah's prophecy, Jesus rode into Jerusalem amid shouts of praise—Hosanna! Save now!—while riding on a donkey.

Jesus knew why he was riding into Jerusalem. The people did not.

Jesus knew what kind of King he was and what kind of King he needed to be. The people did not.

Jesus knew the kind of salvation and freedom he would bring. The people did not.

Not even his disciples understood the significance of this day.

The significance of this day—selection day, a day on which Jewish families were to select the lamb they would sacrifice for the Passover—was that the Passover Lamb was riding into town to be the sacrifice for sin. The significance of this day—a day when Jewish families sang psalms of praise in anticipation of the

Passover—was that they were praising the one whom God had sent to be their Savior-King.

Hosanna! Blessed is he who comes in the name of the Lord! Jesus came to give his life so that we may have life with him in heaven!

*Lord Jesus, may my entire life be a palm branch and a shout of praise that hails you as my Savior-King! Amen.*

## The Word Will Get a Response

### John 12:17-19

*The crowd that was with him when he called Lazarus out of the tomb and raised him from the dead kept telling what they had seen. This is another reason a crowd met him: They heard he had done this miraculous sign.*

*So the Pharisees said to one another, "You see? You are accomplishing nothing. Look! The world has gone after him."*

The Pharisees had made several attempts to silence Jesus and put an end to his popularity. They had asked him leading questions, trying to trip him up and discredit him as a teacher. They questioned his authority and the behavior of his disciples. They had roughed up some of the people whom he had healed, trying to use intimidation as a tactic to keep others from following him or seeking his help. They had given orders that anyone who knew where to find Jesus was to turn him in so that they could arrest him. In the meantime, they plotted his murder. The word about Jesus elicited a response from the

Jewish leaders—they hated him, opposed him, and sought to silence him.

But the word about Jesus elicited the exact opposite response in the hearts of believers—especially on Palm Sunday. They praised Jesus not just with palm branches, cloaks, shouts, and psalm quotes from the Old Testament. They also praised him by telling others who he was and what he had done.

Notice what we can control and what we can't. We can't control how people will respond to the Word about Jesus. We can't control whether they will hate, despise, and oppose him or whether the Holy Spirit will bring them to faith and move them to praise Jesus with their lips. But what we can control is whether we will be the ones to spread the Word about Jesus. May no threat, fear, or intimidation ever keep us from sharing with others the good news of who Jesus is and what he has done to save us.

*Holy Spirit, make me bold to confess my faith. Work through your Word that I share with others so that they may believe in Jesus and receive his forgiveness. Amen.*

---

## The Son Is Glorified

### John 12:20-26

*Now there were some Greeks among those who went up to worship at the Festival. They came to Philip, who was from Bethsaida in Galilee, and asked him, "Sir, we want to see Jesus." Philip went to tell Andrew. Andrew came with Philip and told Jesus.*

*Jesus answered them, "The time has come for the Son of Man to be glorified. Amen, Amen, I tell you: Unless a*

*kernel of wheat falls to the ground and dies, it continues
to be one kernel. But if it dies, it produces much grain.
Anyone who loves his life destroys it. And the one who
hates his life in this world will hold on to it for eternal
life. If anyone serves me, let him follow me. And where I
am, there my servant will be also. If anyone serves me, the
Father will honor him."*

Countless Jews were in Jerusalem to celebrate the Passover.
Some Greek converts to Judaism were also there. They
approached Philip, one of the Twelve—perhaps because he was
the first apostle they saw, perhaps because he had a Greek name
and they felt more comfortable with him, perhaps because he
was from northern Galilee and they knew him—with a request
to see Jesus. Why a request? Were they nervous? Was Jesus just
that busy? Had Jesus made security tight? Was it because they
were Greeks? We don't know. In fact, all we hear about them is
their request. They fade out of the account just as quickly as they
had entered it.

The focus of Jesus' statement is that the hour had finally come
for the Son of Man to be glorified. No more waiting. No more
"now's not the right time." His death and resurrection were only
a few days away. How would he be glorified? This request of the
Greeks is one way. Isaiah had prophesied that the Son of Man
would come, the Savior would come, for all people—not just for
the Jews. Jesus had come also for these Greeks. He was glorified
in the fact that these men came and that he had opportunity to
assure them that he had come to save all people. He was glorified
in the fulfillment of Isaiah's prophecy. He was glorified in the fact
that there would be many more Greeks and Gentiles who would
be brought to faith in him—this was just the beginning.

But, ultimately, the Son of Man would be glorified in his death
that would pay for the world's sins and his resurrection that

would bring life—spiritual and eternal life—to all who believe. Jesus is the seed that died and was buried. Jesus is the seed that brings life—a spiritual harvest—to many. The Son of Man was glorified when the Holy Spirit brought us to faith in him as our only Savior from sin.

*Lord Jesus, use me to bring others to you that they may see you, the Light of the world, and believe that you are the only solution to sin and death. Amen.*

---

# God Is Glorified

### John 12:27-29

> *"Now my soul is troubled. And what shall I say? 'Father, save me from this hour'? No, this is the reason I came to this hour. Father, glorify your name!"*
> *A voice came from heaven: "I have glorified my name, and I will glorify it again."*
> *The crowd standing there heard it and said it thundered. Others said an angel talked to him.*

The palm branches and shouts of praise did not cause Jesus to lose focus. All the attention, all the cloaks in his path, did not distract Jesus to the point where he forgot why he had come to earth in the first place. As Jesus rode into Jerusalem on a donkey, he was well aware that he would soon die, but he would do more than just die. He would face a pain and a suffering worse than crucifixion. He would suffer hell. He would endure God's wrath and punishment—not because of anything he had done but because of everything we have done. While this thought troubled him, it did not cause him to jump ship. Jesus knew that this was the very reason he had come to earth. He came to die. He came to pay for sin. He came to take our punishment upon himself. He came to save us. And this salvation would bring glory to God the Father. Jesus' death on the cross brought glory to God the Father because it was the only way God could satisfy both his justice and his love—his justice that demanded payment for sin and his love that wants all to be saved. Only on the cross of Jesus do we see both being satisfied. Only because of the cross—because of Jesus' death on the cross—do we have God's forgiveness and pardon.

*Heavenly Father, may I bring glory to your name by telling others of your gracious plan in Christ to save us from sin. Amen.*

---

## Only Through the Cross

### John 12:30-36

*Jesus answered, "This voice was not for my sake but for yours.*

*"Now is the judgment of this world. Now the ruler of this world will be thrown out. And I, when I am lifted up from the earth, will draw all people to myself." He said this to indicate what kind of death he was going to die.*

*The crowd answered him, "We have heard from the Scriptures that the Christ will remain forever. So how can you say, 'The Son of Man must be lifted up'? Who is this Son of Man?"*

*Then Jesus told them, "The light will be with you just a little while longer. Keep on walking while you have the light, so that darkness does not overtake you. The one who*

*walks in the darkness does not know where he is going.*
*While you have the light, believe in the light, so that you*
*may become sons of light."*

*Jesus spoke these words, and then went away and was*
*hidden from them.*

It was Holy Week. Jesus had already ridden into Jerusalem on a donkey to shouts of praise. The people acknowledged that he was the Son of David. But what did that mean? At the time, the crowds thought it meant the time for freedom, the time for restoration, the time for an earthly messianic kingdom had come. Yet Jesus dashed all such hopes, dreams, and thoughts when he said he was going to be "lifted up." They caught the reference to crucifixion. They wondered how Jesus could be the Christ and rule forever here on earth if he were to be lifted up and killed.

But it was through that very death on the cross that Jesus would confirm his role as the Messiah and establish his eternal kingdom. It is only through his cross that Jesus brings us into his kingdom. It is only through his cross that Jesus offers us for-giveness, life, and salvation. It is only through his cross that Jesus reveals who he is—the Son of Man born to save humankind. It is only through his cross that the gospel sheds light on our hearts. The crowds would only have Jesus—the Light of the world—among them a few more days, and then he would die (and rise!). Jesus called them to put their trust in him for salvation while he was still among them. The light of Jesus continues to shine on us through the gospel. The gospel enables us not simply to walk in the light of Jesus but to bask in the light of faith, knowledge, hope, understanding, forgiveness, life, and salvation.

*How grateful I am, Jesus, that you have shed your light on me*
*through the gospel. Thank you. Thank you for the eyes of faith that*
*see my salvation in your death on the cross. Amen.*

# What About Me?

**John 12:37-43**

*Even though Jesus had done so many miraculous signs in their presence, they still did not believe in him. This was to fulfill the word of Isaiah the prophet, who said: "Lord, who has believed our message? And to whom has the arm of the Lord been revealed?"*

*For this reason they could not believe, because Isaiah also said: "He has blinded their eyes and hardened their heart, so that they would not see with their eyes, or understand with their heart, or turn—and I would heal them."*

*Isaiah said these things when he saw Jesus' glory and spoke about him.*

*Nevertheless, even many of the rulers believed in him, but because of the Pharisees they were not confessing him, so that they would not be put out of the synagogue. For they loved praise from people more than praise from God.*

All on their own, entirely on their own, the Pharisees had rejected Jesus. Their spiritually blind eyes refused to see him as the promised Messiah. God let them have their way. As he did with Pharaoh after his repeated defiance and rejection (which he entirely did on his own when God finally said enough was enough and hardened Pharaoh's unbelieving heart), so God did with these Pharisees. He confirmed them in their spiritual blindness. He let them have it their way. They didn't want to see Jesus as their Savior; God saw to it, then, that they would never see Jesus as their Savior—and all this in fulfillment of Isaiah's prophecy. That is a harsh yet just judgment—one we dare not take lightly.

By God's grace, some of the people—including some of these Pharisees, these leaders—did believe that Jesus was the Messiah. God had given them the eyes of faith to see Jesus as their Savior. Intimidation and fear allowed the old Adam, however, to win the day—they did not confess their faith in Jesus openly. Respect and praise from their own people were more important to them than God.

What about me—what about you? By God's grace he has given us the eyes of faith to see Jesus as our Savior. By God's grace he has taken our stone-cold, dead, and unbelieving hearts and brought them to life. By God's grace he has not blinded our eyes or hardened our hearts in judgment. We are not these Pharisees; we are not Pharaoh, but let's also not be the intimidated and fear-filled believers in this account. Let us boldly confess our faith in and our allegiance to our one and only Savior from sin—both in what we say and what we do.

*Keep me in your Word, dear Jesus, that the Holy Spirit may keep me spiritually alive, that my heart would never become hard, that my eyes would never be blinded to you, and that my tongue may always confess your name. Amen.*

---

## Saving Faith

### John 12:44-46

*Then Jesus called out, "The one who believes in me does not believe in me only, but in him who sent me. And the one who sees me sees him who sent me. I have come into the world as a light, so that everyone who believes in me would not remain in darkness."*

Jesus has called us out of darkness into his wonderful light.

Jesus has called us out of the darkness of unbelief, ignorance, denial, confusion, impenitence, and opposition. He has called us into the light of faith, knowledge, acceptance, wisdom, penitence, and fellowship.

Jesus has given us faith—saving faith.

Saving faith certainly includes trusting in Jesus as our one and only Savior. Saving faith also includes a knowledge of who Jesus is—true God and true man in one person born to be our substitute in life and death, the one who lived perfectly in our place to make us righteous through faith in him and endured our just punishment on the cross to pay for our sin so that God may forgive us.

But in these verses, Jesus reminds us that saving faith includes more than just a knowledge of who he is and what he has done. It includes more than trusting in him for salvation. Saving faith includes a knowledge of the Father and the Holy Spirit. Saving faith includes trusting in the triune God for salvation. By his grace alone, the triune God has given us this saving faith to know him, believe in him, and trust in him.

*Help me, Holy Spirit, not simply to remain in faith but to grow in my faith, knowing that it is through faith in Jesus—and in the Trinity—that I am saved. Do this through your means of grace as you have promised. Amen.*

# Who Will Judge?

### John 12:47-50

*"If anyone hears my words but does not hold on to them, I do not judge him, for I did not come to judge the world, but to save the world. The one who rejects me and does not receive my words does have a judge. The word which I spoke is what will judge him on the Last Day, because I have not spoken on my own, but the Father himself who sent me has given me a command regarding what I am to say and what I am to speak. And I know that his command is eternal life. So the things I speak are exactly what the Father told me to speak."*

Jesus came to shine the light of the gospel on the darkness of the world's unbelief. Jesus came to testify to the truth. Jesus came to share the message his Father had given him to share.

While we do confess in the Apostles' Creed that Jesus will come again to judge the living and the dead—and while Scripture most certainly does teach this truth—Jesus here informs us that he ultimately is not the one who will judge the world. He came to save the world; he came to live a life of obedience for the world; he came to die a sacrificial death for the world; he came to defeat death with his own resurrection from the dead and give that victory to the world; he came to fulfill and proclaim the gospel; yes, Jesus came to save the world.

But if Jesus isn't the one who will ultimately judge the world, who will? The very Word that Jesus both fulfilled and proclaimed will judge the people of the world. Those who reject the Word reject Jesus. The Word they rejected will condemn them. The Word will say, "You did not believe me. You did not believe what I said about Jesus. You did not heed my call to repentance. You did not see in my pages your substitute and Savior Jesus. And for all this you stand condemned."

Dear Christian, thank Jesus for his Word! Thank Jesus that his Word is the power of God for the salvation of all who believe. Thank Jesus that faith comes from hearing the message and the message is heard through the Word of Christ. Thank God that in your life God's Word did not return to him empty but accomplished the purpose for which he sent it—namely, to bring you to faith in Jesus so that you will not stand condemned on the Last Day.

*Dear Jesus, thank you for letting the gospel be the power of God for the salvation of all who believe. Amen.*

---

# He Came to Serve

### John 13:1-5

*Before the Passover Festival, Jesus knew that the time had come for him to leave this world and go to the Father. Having loved those who were his own in the world, he loved them to the end.*

*By the time the supper took place, the Devil had already put the idea into the heart of Judas, son of Simon Iscariot, to betray Jesus.*

*Jesus knew that the Father had given all things into his hands, and that he had come from God and was going back to God. He got up from the supper and laid aside his outer garment. He took a towel and tied it around his waist. Then he poured water into a basin and began to wash his disciples' feet, drying them with the towel that was wrapped around him.*

It was Holy Week. More than that, it was the night before Jesus' death. It was Passover. And what do we see the Passover Lamb (literally hours before being whipped, beaten, and crucified) doing? Humbling himself in love to serve those who were too proud to serve each other and too ignorant to serve the eternal Son of God who was sitting among them.

Jesus knew everything that was about to happen to him—the betrayal, the trials, the mocking, the abuse, the pain, the torture, the death—and his thought was not of himself and his needs but on his disciples and their needs. In an object lesson, the eternal Son of God—the master teacher, the Lord, the Messiah—got down on his hands and knees to wash the feet of his disciples like a common servant. Humble service. Loving service. Service that doesn't even compare to the way he would serve them the very next day by giving his life as a ransom for sin.

Jesus hasn't washed our feet, but he has served us in love. He humbled himself and became obedient to death on the cross. He died in our place. He paid for our sins. And in Baptism he washed not just our feet but our entire being. In Baptism he washed our sins away so that we may stand clean—holy and blameless—before God.

*Jesus, help me to humbly serve in love those around me as a way of expressing my gratitude for the humble, loving way that you served me. Amen.*

# He Had to Serve

**John 13:6-9**

> *He came to Simon Peter, who asked him, "Lord, are you going to wash my feet?"*
>
> *Jesus answered him, "You do not understand what I am doing now, but later you will understand."*
>
> *Peter told him, "You will never, ever, wash my feet!"*
>
> *Jesus replied, "If I do not wash you, you have no part with me."*
>
> *"Lord, not just my feet," Simon Peter replied, "but also my hands and my head!"*

Peter. You gotta love him. A man of knee-jerk reactions. A man of overreactions.

Peter was not comfortable with Jesus washing his feet. This service was beneath his master. He shouldn't have had to stoop so low—to humiliate himself in this way. "You will never, ever, wash my feet!" And yet, Peter didn't grab the towel and basin and start washing everyone's feet in place of Jesus either.

Jesus told Peter that unless he washed his feet, Peter would have no part with him. The pendulum swings. "Not just my feet . . . but also my hands and my head!" The whole body!

Peter didn't understand that the humble service of foot washing was a prelude to the humble service of his master's suffering and death on the cross. Peter didn't understand that the washing Jesus had in mind had nothing to do with feet, hands, or heads; it had nothing to do with a towel and a basin of water but everything to do with his blood that he would shed the very next day to wash away the sins of the world. That is the service, the humble service, that makes us clean; it is because of that service that we have any part with Jesus.

*Thank you, Jesus, for washing away my sins with your death on the cross and welcoming me into your family through the waters of Baptism. Amen.*

---

## Who's Clean?

### John 13:10,11

*Jesus told him, "A person who has had a bath needs only to wash his feet, but his body is completely clean. And you are clean, but not all of you." Indeed, he knew who was going to betray him. That is why he said, "Not all of you are clean."*

People who walked the dusty roads of Judea wearing only sandals on their feet needed to wash those feet regularly. In fact, washing the feet of your guests when they arrived at your home became a custom and a common courtesy often extended. Notice, though, that the traveler who had bathed or washed up before leaving his home needed only to have his feet washed when he arrived; he didn't need to wash his entire body. Jesus reiterated that point for Peter, who had swung the pendulum too far.

In one sentence, however, Jesus switched from a literal washing to a spiritual washing; he switched from dusty dirt to sinful grime, from water-washed feet to blood-washed souls. His disciples were clean—through faith in their Savior they had been washed free from sin; through faith in Jesus they stood holy and blameless before God, as a beautiful bride without stain or wrinkle or any other blemish. Though not every one of them was clean—Jesus was referring to Judas, who, for selfish motives and greedy gain, would betray him. Judas had refused to believe in Jesus. Judas had refused the cleansing shower of God's grace. His sin remained. His sin condemned.

Who's clean? All those who believe in Jesus are clean. You are clean. I am clean. Look no further than the baptismal font to know that's true. Baptism is the shortest bath we've ever had, but it is the bath that has made us the cleanest we will ever be. Through it, Jesus washed away our sin and robed us in his righteousness.

*Clean through faith in you, dear Jesus, help me to daily drown my old Adam in contrition and repentance so that each day a new person may arise, as from the dead, to live before you in true righteousness and holiness. Amen.*

---

## No Service Is Beneath Me

**John 13:12-17**

*After Jesus had washed their feet and put on his outer garment, he reclined at the table again. "Do you understand what I have done for you?" he asked them. "You call me Teacher and Lord. You are right, because I am. Now if I, your Lord and Teacher, have washed your feet, you also ought to wash one another's feet. Yes, I have given you an example so that you also would do just as I have done for you. Amen, Amen, I tell you: A servant is not greater than his master, nor is a messenger greater than the one who sent him. If you know these things, you are blessed if you do them."*

The one who was in a position of authority over the disciples—their Lord and teacher, their master and leader—taught them true leadership through his humble attitude and service.

It is often said that those who coach a team coach like those who coached them, those who teach a class teach like those who taught them, and those who lead a group lead like those who led them.

Oh, that this may apply to us and our coach, teacher, and leader! May we follow his lead! May we humbly serve others as he humbly served us! May we model his servantlike attitude in our relationship with others! Whether we talk about our roles as parents, spouses, children, students, employees, or members of a local church, may we, like Jesus, not only say but also demonstrate that no service is beneath us!

*Jesus, you served me by giving your life as a ransom for sin. Empower and motivate me to serve you by offering a humble life of service to those around me. Amen.*

---

## So That You Will Know

### John 13:18-20

*"I am not talking about all of you. I know those I have chosen. But this is so that the Scripture may be fulfilled: 'One who eats bread with me has raised his heel against me.' I am telling you this right now before it happens, so that when it does happen, you may believe that I am he.*

*"Amen, Amen, I tell you: Whoever receives anyone I send, receives me. And whoever receives me, receives the one who sent me."*

Jesus had just washed the disciples' feet. Jesus had just told Peter that he was spiritually clean. But now some startling news—not every one of them was clean. There was one among them who did not love Jesus, did not believe in Jesus, and did not trust in Jesus as his Savior. This one would betray Jesus. Startling news. Why did Jesus share it? So that when they saw it happen, they would believe in him all the more. Think of that. This prophecy about the one who would betray him would serve to strengthen their faith!

Jesus knew everything that would happen to him. Jesus was in complete control of everything that would happen to him. And he let it happen anyway! He let it happen because of those whom he had chosen—because of you and me. Jesus chose us! Think of that! He did not choose us because of anything we did or would do, because of anything we are or would be, or because he knew we would believe in him. No, he chose us in spite of the sinful things we do, in spite of the sinners we are, in spite of the fact that we could not believe in him on our own. He chose us to be his and then, in time, through his life and death and resurrection, through faith that the Holy Spirit gives, he made us his own; he made us holy and blameless. We are his. He wants us to know that. He wants us to be assured of that.

*Holy Spirit, assure me every day that I belong to Jesus and that through faith in Jesus I have both his forgiveness and his righteousness so that I may stand holy and blameless before my heavenly Father. Amen.*

# Do It Quickly

### John 13:21-30

*After saying this, Jesus was troubled in his spirit
and testified, "Amen, Amen, I tell you: One of you will
betray me."*

*The disciples were looking at each other, uncertain
which of them he meant.*

*One of his disciples, the one Jesus loved, was reclining
at Jesus' side. So Simon Peter motioned to him to find out
which one he was talking about.*

*So leaning back against Jesus' side, he asked, "Lord,
who is it?"*

*Jesus replied, "It is the one to whom I will give this
piece of bread, after I have dipped it in the dish." Then he
dipped the piece of bread and gave it to Judas, the son of
Simon Iscariot. As soon as Judas took the bread, Satan
entered into him.*

*So Jesus told him, "What you are about to do, do
more quickly."*

*None of those reclining at the table understood why
Jesus said this to him. Because Judas kept the money box,
some thought that Jesus was telling him, "Buy what we
need for the Festival," or to give something to the poor. As
soon as Judas had taken the bread, he went out. And it
was night.*

What surprises you most as you read these words? What
amazes you most as you read these words?

Is it the honest and straightforward way that Jesus spoke with
his disciples as he plainly laid out the truth that one of them
would betray him?

Is it the ripple of "Surely not I, Lord?" that coursed through the hearts, minds, and mouths of the disciples?

Is it the love of Jesus that reached out to Judas through the piece of bread he extended to him—a gesture of honoring a special guest at a meal?

Is it the call to repentance found in such a gesture?

Is it the ability of Judas to betray his Lord for 30 pieces of silver?

Is it the statement that Satan entered Judas and took control of his heart and actions?

Is it the fact that Judas left to carry out the betrayal Jesus clearly knew was coming?

Is it the naïveté of the disciples about what just happened?

Maybe.

But isn't the most surprising and amazing part of this account the fact that Jesus urged Judas to do what he was about to do and to do it quickly? In a sense, isn't it amazing that Jesus was hastening his betrayal, which would set in motion his trials, all the abuse, his crucifixion, and, ultimately, his death? That's the love and commitment of our Savior in action. He knew why he had come to the earth, so he did and said whatever was necessary to fulfill God's plan of salvation and even hasten his death now that the hour of his death was upon him.

*Lord, keep me faithful to you. Through Word and sacrament, help me keep you my number one priority in life. Amen.*

## Let Them Know

### John 13:31-35

*After Judas left, Jesus said, "Now the Son of Man is glorified, and God is glorified in him. If God is glorified in him, God will also glorify the Son in himself and will glorify him at once.*

*"Dear children, I am going to be with you only a little longer. You will look for me, and just as I told the Jews, so I tell you now: Where I am going, you cannot come.*

*"A new commandment I give you: Love one another. Just as I have loved you, so also you are to love one another. By this everyone will know that you are my disciples, if you have love for one another."*

Jesus had already gotten down on his hands and knees to wash his disciples' feet—a humble act of love and service, one they were to follow in their own lives of faith. Judas had already gotten up from the table to leave the upper room—a traitorous act of greed and betrayal.

The table is now set for God to be glorified—both the Father and the Son—but not in any way that anyone would have ever predicted or anticipated. God the Father would be glorified in the willing and determined obedience of his Son. And the Son would be glorified on a cross—in his suffering and death that would pay for the sins of the world.

This he would do alone. This no one could do with him—not the disciples, not us, not anyone. Only he—only Jesus, the Lamb of God—could pay for the sins of the world. And only he, the one who loved us enough to take our place under the punishing hand of our heavenly Father, is the one who can—and does—freely forgive us all our sins.

So now what—now that Jesus glorified his Father by laying down his life for our sins, the Father glorified his Son by exalting him to the highest place and giving him the name that is above all names, and we are fully and forgiven by the Father in the Son? Now that we are fully and freely forgiven by the Father in the Son? Simple! Love. Love one another. Love as he has loved us. We glorify God in our humble acts of love and service—acts of love and service that reveal our identity as children of God.

*Lord Jesus, let my light of faith shine before others that they may see my deeds of love and praise my Father in heaven. Amen.*

---

## Committed

### John 13:36-38

> *Simon Peter said to him, "Lord, where are you going?"*
> *Jesus answered, "Where I am going you cannot follow now, but you will follow later."*
> *Peter asked, "Lord, why can't I follow you now? I will lay down my life for you!"*
> *Jesus replied, "Will you really lay down your life for me? Amen, Amen, I tell you: The rooster will not crow until you have denied me three times."*

A four-year-old girl in Sunday school during our lesson on Adam and Eve and the fall into sin once told me that if she were Eve, she never would have eaten that piece of fruit. At such a young age, she clearly loved her Lord and clearly wanted to obey him. Love. Commitment. Desire. Dedication. From a four-year-old.

What about Peter? "I will lay down my life for you!" Love. Commitment. Desire. Dedication. Sure, absolutely. But a bit naïve? A little overconfident? Self-reliant? Foolish? Yes. Sadly, the night played out just as Jesus said it would. The rooster did crow and, far worse, Peter did disown Jesus three times.

If you think you are standing firm, be careful that you do not fall (see 1 Corinthians 10:12). Temptations will come in seemingly innocent things: a piece of fruit in a beautiful garden, an innocent question from a young girl in a courtyard. Temptations will come. Let's not be naïve about that. But when they do come, let's not put our confidence in our strength; let's not rely on ourselves; let's not foolishly say or think that we won't give in. Rather, when we are tempted, let's look for the ways out that God has promised us. Let's say to those temptations what Jesus said to the tempter in the wilderness: "It is written!" Let's wield the sword of God's truth and cut through the lies of Satan. Let's stand firm in Christ.

But when we—like Eve, like Peter, like that four-year-old Sunday school student—fall, Jesus is right there to pick us up, build us up, and assure us that he laid down his life for us—only to take it up again. He is right there to forgive us. Jesus will always have more forgiveness than we have sin, and he will always have more grace than we have guilt.

*God, you are faithful. You have promised that you will not let me be tempted beyond what I can bear and that when I am tempted, you will provide a way out so that I can stand up under it. Lord, provide that way out and help me not only see it but also make use of it. But when I fall, pick me up and forgive me in Jesus. Amen.*

# The Place Has Already Been Prepared

### John 14:1-4

*"Do not let your heart be troubled. Believe in God; believe also in me. In my Father's house are many mansions. If it were not so, I would have told you. I am going to prepare a place for you. And if I go and prepare a place for you, I will come again and take you to be with me, so that you may also be where I am. You know where I am going, and you know the way."*

The night before his death Jesus had been honest with his disciples. His talk of betrayal had upset and troubled them. He began to comfort them. And he continues to comfort us. How? By telling us about the mansions in his Father's house (heaven) that he has prepared for us. By assuring us that he will come back to take us there. By telling us that we already know the way to the place where he is going. He is the Way. He is also the Truth and the Life.

Jesus prepared this place for us in his Father's house the very next day. He built those rooms for us in heaven at the lumberyard of Calvary where he used only two pieces of blood-stained wood and three flesh-piercing nails. Jesus' death on the cross prepared heaven for us. Our sin had kept us out of heaven. His death paid for our sin. With sin atoned for—through Jesus—the way to heaven is free and open to all. What comfort! The place is already prepared. What hope! Jesus is coming back. What joy! We will live with him forever.

*Lord, do not let my heart be troubled. When my conscience troubles me, assure me of your forgiveness. When the world frightens me, remind me of heaven. When worry consumes me, fill me with trust. Amen.*

## We Know the Way

### John 14:5-7

*"Lord, we don't know where you are going," Thomas replied, "so how can we know the way?"*

*Jesus said to him, "I am the Way and the Truth and the Life. No one comes to the Father, except through me. If you know me, you would also know my Father. From now on you do know him and have seen him."*

The night before his death Jesus had told his disciples that he was going to prepare a place for them and would come back to take them there so that they could be there with him.

Put yourself in the disciples' shoes for just a minute. Jesus hadn't been betrayed yet. Jesus hadn't been put on trial yet. Jesus hadn't been handed over to be crucified yet. Though Jesus had told them several times everything that was going to happen to him, the disciples still had no clue what would happen to Jesus over the next 24 hours. They had no clue what he meant when he told them that he was going away but would come back. Are you going to Capernaum? Are you going to Galilee? Are you going to a quiet place to pray? Are you going to Mary and Martha's house? Are you checking in with Lazarus? Are you going somewhere to make preparations for our next mission trip? These would all be possible thoughts and conclusions in light of what Jesus had said and the knowledge the disciples had at the time.

None are what Jesus meant, however. Jesus was talking about going to heaven. He was talking about preparing a place for them there and coming back to take them and all believers home to heaven. And while they didn't know the way (because they didn't know where he was going), Jesus told them that they did know the way—he was (he is) the way to the Father, the way to heaven.

We know the way because we know Jesus. We know the way to heaven—it is through Jesus, through the life he lived in our place, and through his death on the cross that paid for our sins. Jesus is coming back, and when he does come back, he will take us and all who believe in him home to heaven.

*Lord, no map is needed; you have given me faith. You are the way to heaven. Thank you, Jesus, for making yourself known to me that I may join you there. Amen.*

---

## We Have Seen the Father

**John 14:8-14**

*"Lord," said Philip, "show us the Father, and that is enough for us."*

*"Have I been with you so long," Jesus answered, "and you still do not know me, Philip? The one who has seen me has seen the Father. How can you say, 'Show us the Father'? Don't you believe that I am in the Father and the Father is in me? The words that I am telling you I am not speaking on my own, but the Father who remains in me is doing his works. Believe me that I am in the Father, and the Father is in me. Or else believe because of the works themselves.*

*"Amen, Amen, I tell you: The one who believes in me will do the works that I am doing. And he will do even greater works than these, because I am going to the Father. I will do whatever you ask in my name so that the Father may be glorified in the Son. If you ask me for anything in my name, I will do it."*

The relationship between God the Father and God the Son goes beyond our human understanding. The inner workings and relationships within the Trinity go beyond our human understanding. Take comfort in that. Our God is greater than we are.

But this we do know—when we look at Jesus, we see the Father. No, Jesus is not the Father, but we can see the Father when we look at the Son. When we look at Jesus, we see God himself. Jesus is God. The Father is present. We see the Father when we look at Jesus because in Jesus we see the Father's plan of salvation, we see the Father's will being carried out, and we hear the Father's Word being shared. The plan was the Father's. The cross was the Father's wisdom—that one would die for all so that all might be saved—but the Son carried out the plan. The Son humbled himself and became obedient to death.

And now, greater than the miracles the disciples saw and performed, we see God the Holy Spirit using God's Word at work in us and our witnessing, bringing people to faith in Jesus. A miracle far greater than restoring physical sight, the Holy Spirit gives eyes of faith. A miracle far greater than raising someone from the dead, the Holy Spirit gives spiritual life to those born spiritually dead. All this brings glory to the Father. All this—the work of God the Son and the work of God the Spirit—shows us the Father's love.

*Thank you, triune God, that though I may not understand just who you are, I know by faith what you did to save me from sin. Amen.*

# We're Not Alone

### John 14:15-21

*"If you love me, hold on to my commands. I will ask the Father, and he will give you another Counselor to be with you forever. He is the Spirit of truth, whom the world cannot receive because it does not see him or know him. You know him because he stays with you and will be in you.*

*"I will not leave you as orphans; I am coming to you. In a little while the world will see me no longer, but you will see me. Because I live, you also will live. In that day you will know that I am in my Father, and you in me, and I in you. The one who has my commands and holds on to them is the one who loves me. And the one who loves me will be loved by my Father. I too will love him and show myself to him."*

Jesus had been with his disciples for three years. Let's not discount the bond and the relationship that had developed between Jesus and his disciples over that time. They had grown to love him. They had grown to depend on him. They had grown used to having him around. Jesus knew that. He also knew that he was leaving them. More than his death and resurrection, Jesus was looking ahead to his ascension. While he would be with them always, it would be different. He would not be among them physically, visibly. Like a parent in the military who is called up and sent overseas, Jesus was leaving his children behind. Imagine the pain, the agony, on both sides. But Jesus wasn't leaving them alone. He promised to send another Counselor—another teacher. He promised to send them the Holy Spirit. He kept that promise on the Day of Pentecost.

He kept that promise to you and me at the baptismal font. In our baptisms, Jesus sent us the same Spirit, the Spirit of truth, the Holy Spirit. The Holy Spirit made us spiritually alive. The Holy Spirit gave us his gift of faith in Jesus. The Holy Spirit continues to counsel and teach us in the Word of God. The Holy Spirit is the one who assures us that we are not alone—that he is with us and Jesus is with us always. He is the one who assures us that Jesus is coming back to take us to be with him in the mansions he has prepared for us. You are never alone! Jesus has given us the greatest Counselor—the Holy Spirit—who assures us that Jesus, our crucified, risen, and ascended Savior, is with us always and we will be with him always and forever in heaven.

*Be with me always, Jesus, as you have promised, that I may never be overwhelmed by loneliness. Amen.*

---

## How Will Others Know

### John 14:22-27

*Judas (not Iscariot) said to him, "Lord, what has happened that you are going to show yourself to us and not to the world?"*

*Jesus answered him, "If anyone loves me, he will hold on to my word. My Father will love him, and we will come to him and make our home with him. The one who does not love me does not hold on to my words. The word that you are hearing is not mine, but it is from the Father who sent me.*

*"I have told you these things while staying with you. But the Counselor, the Holy Spirit, whom the Father will*

*send in my name, will teach you all things and remind*
*you of everything I told you.*

*"Peace I leave with you. My peace I give to you. Not as*
*the world gives do I give to you. Do not let your heart be*
*troubled, and do not let it be afraid."*

At first glance it doesn't seem as though Jesus answered Judas' question. It seems as though Jesus just rambled on, talking about something totally different. This would especially seem to be the case if the disciples were still thinking that Jesus was going to establish an earthly kingdom. Then Judas' question becomes perfectly clear. "How can you reign on a throne here on earth and drive out the Romans and rule the people in peace if you go away and never reveal yourself as the people's king?" Understanding that Jesus proceeded to answer his question in terms of his spiritual kingdom reveals that Jesus didn't change the subject or ramble on about something irrelevant to the question but rather that Jesus went on to explain how his spiritual kingdom would grow and the type of peace his people would enjoy.

The disciples were confused, and Jesus knew it—even though he had been speaking frankly with them. Jesus told them again that he would send a Counselor, the Holy Spirit, who would remind them of everything Jesus had just told them but that he would do so in light of everything Jesus was about to do—his suffering, death, and resurrection. The Holy Spirit would come. The Holy Spirit would work in their hearts. The Holy Spirit would bring them understanding. The Holy Spirit would bring them peace, they in turn would bring peace to others, and others in turn would bring peace to us. The kingdom of God grows one Christian at a time. The kingdom of God grows whenever the Holy Spirit brings someone to faith in Jesus and showers that person's guilty conscience with the peace of sins forgiven and the assurance that all is well with God because of Jesus.

*Lord Jesus, use me to share your Spirit and peace with others by moving me to share your Word and teaching with others. Let your kingdom come. Amen.*

---

# We Want This to Happen

### John 14:28-31

*"You heard me tell you, 'I am going away, and I am coming to you.' If you loved me, you would be glad that I am going to the Father, because the Father is greater than I.*

*"I have told you now before it happens so that, when it does happen, you may believe. I will not speak with you much longer, because the ruler of this world is coming. He has no power over me. But I want the world to know that I love the Father and that I am doing exactly what the Father has instructed me."*

*"Get up. Let's leave this place."*

"You want me to go away."

"You need me to go away."

"You don't understand this now, but you will."

The fact that Jesus was going away meant several things. It started with his betrayal; it continued with his trials. It culminated on the cross when Jesus died—he literally went away. For three days he went away from them as his dead body lay in the tomb. Then he came back—he came back to life; he came back to them, only to go away again. Forty days after his resurrection, he ascended into heaven; he returned to the Father.

But both he and the Father wanted this to happen—they wanted Jesus to go away; Jesus wanted to die. He wanted to pay for the sins of the world. Though Satan had a hold on him, Jesus was the one who let all this happen—his suffering and death, the atonement of the world's sins. He and the Father were in complete agreement; they both wanted this to happen. After all, Jesus and the Father—in the mystery of the Trinity—are one.

But we wanted this to happen too. No, we did not want to see Jesus die—we did not want him to go away in that way—but we needed him to. We needed him to pay for our sins, but God did not let him go away in death for long—only three days. Then he came back. And now that he has ascended, as much as we would love to walk and talk with Jesus today as the disciples had back then, we needed him to go away so that he can return once again just as he promised to take us all home to heaven on the Last Day.

*Keep me always watchful, always prepared, Lord, for your sudden but joyful return. Amen.*

## Remain in Me

### John 15:1-4

*"I am the true vine, and my Father is the gardener. Every branch in me that does not bear fruit, he is going to cut off. And he prunes every branch that does bear fruit, so that it will bear more fruit.*

*"You are already clean because of the word I have spoken to you. Remain in me, and I am going to remain in you. A branch cannot bear fruit by itself; it must*

*remain in the vine. Likewise, you cannot bear fruit unless*
*you remain in me."*

How simple and clear.

Jesus is the vine. We are the branches. The vine gives life to the branches. Live branches bear fruit. Jesus is the one who gives us this spiritual life. Jesus empowers and motivates our faith to produce fruit. Quite simply, connected to Jesus, we will bear fruit.

At times we branches need to be pruned. The gardener prunes the branches on the vine so that the branches will be healthier and able to produce bigger and better fruit. Our heavenly gardener is constantly using his law and gospel to prune us and our lives. As we grow in our faith, as we mature in our faith—as he, through Spirit-worked repentance, cuts out our sinful attitudes, words, and actions—there is more room for and more ability to produce fruits of the heart, mouth, and body that are in keeping with God's will and that bring him glory.

At times, however, rather than simply pruning a branch, the gardener will need to cut off an entire branch because it has died. It serves no purpose. It is merely giving the impression that it is connected to the vine. Our heavenly gardener must, at times, cut off dead, unbelieving branches to make more room for new, living branches.

A warning? To be sure. The application? Jesus said it. Remain in me. How? How do we remain in Jesus? How do we stay connected to Jesus the vine so that we remain alive, so that we can avoid being cut off and thrown into the fire, so that we can be pruned, and so that we can continue to produce fruit? Word and sacrament. Worship. Devotion. Bible study. Our faith is fed only through the means of grace.

*Holy Spirit, through Word and sacrament, keep me connected*
*to Jesus that I may remain in him, the vine. Keep me alive and*
*growing. Enable me to produce fruit. Help me to make the most*

*of every opportunity before me to hear, learn, and study your Word. Amen.*

## What's on Your Branches?

### John 15:5-8

*"I am the Vine; you are the branches. The one who remains in me and I in him is the one who bears much fruit, because without me you can do nothing. If anyone does not remain in me, he is thrown away like a branch and withers. Such branches are gathered, thrown into the fire, and burned. If you remain in me and my words remain in you, ask whatever you wish, and it will be done for you. My Father is glorified by this: that you continue to bear much fruit and prove to be my disciples."*

Dead branches are cut off a tree as the tree is pruned. Those dead branches are picked up and thrown into the woodchipper or onto the bonfire and are burned.

Spiritually dead branches experience an even worse fate—they are cut off from the vine of Christ and thrown into the fires of hell. Before those branches died, however, they had stopped producing fruit; they had begun to wither. They died because they were not being fed the life-giving water of the Word. Certainly, this is a warning for us. None of us wants to be cut off and thrown into the fire of hell, but we have better motivation than fear to keep us connected to Christ and his Word. We have opportunities to bear much fruit, beautiful and delicious fruit, that not only reveal that we are Jesus' disciples but also bring glory to God. Each fruit that our faith produces is a personalized thank-you card to the God who loves, forgives, and saves us.

The owner of an orchard does not need to walk up and down the rows of apple trees each morning and order the trees to produce apples. Those trees just naturally produce apples. The healthier the trees, the better the apples. May our fruits of faith be just as natural and just as healthy—produced not out of fear of hell but rather out of thanksgiving for heaven.

*May my branches, Lord, be filled with God-pleasing fruits that bring you glory. Amen.*

## Love Each Other

### John 15:9-13

*"As the Father has loved me, so also I have loved you. Remain in my love. If you hold on to my commands, you will remain in my love, just as I have held on to my Father's commands and remain in his love. I have told you these things so that my joy would continue to be in you and that your joy would be complete.*

*"This is my command: Love one another as I have loved you. No one has greater love than this: that someone lays down his life for his friends."*

Jesus wasn't asking us to do something he hasn't already done.

This is his command: "Love one another," and he adds, "as I have loved you."

Okay.

Right? How can we not, in turn, love one another? How can we not put other people and their needs and feelings ahead of our own? How can we not make personal sacrifices that will be of great help to others?

We know what Jesus has done for us! We know the lengths to which he was willing to go—the lengths to which he went—in order to save us from our sin. Jesus laid down his life for his friends—the ultimate sacrifice. The blood he shed covered our lack of love. His death on the cross canceled our every failure to love and put others first. Jesus showed his love for the Father by obeying his Father's commands, which included laying down his life for the sins of the world.

Our joy is complete when we understand and appreciate Jesus' love for us and when we respond to that love by loving others and obeying his commands. The love we show others and our obedience to Jesus' commands bring the Savior who died for us great joy.

"Love one another as I have loved you."

Okay.

*Lord, make my joy complete by helping me find joy in serving— and loving—others. Amen.*

---

## Love One Another

**John 15:14-17**

*"You are my friends if you continue to do the things I instruct you. I no longer call you servants, because a servant does not know what his master is doing. But I have called you friends, because everything that I heard*

*from my Father, I have made known to you. You did not choose me, but I chose you and appointed you to go and bear fruit, fruit that will endure, so that the Father will give you whatever you ask in my name. These things I am instructing you, so that you love one another."*

Remember when we said that the owner of the apple orchard doesn't need to walk up and down his rows of apple trees and tell each tree, "Produce apples!"? It is natural for an apple tree to produce apples.

How simple, then—how obvious—when Jesus tells you and me, "Love one another." Why wouldn't we? Because it's not natural. Showing love is not natural to our human nature. Our human nature is selfish, defensive, and guarded. Our human nature wants to be served; it doesn't want to serve. It should surprise none of us that it is not natural for us to love one another—it is difficult for us to show love to one another because often we are too concerned about loving ourselves.

But what did Jesus do? He is the vine, isn't he? He grafted us into him. He changed our status—no longer are we servants; we are his friends. He chose us. He brought us to faith in him. He forgives our sins because of his death. He empowers us to live because of his resurrection. He made his Father's will known to us—and that will is to love him and one another. As friends of Jesus who know his Father's will, we have the right to ask of him anything we wish—but what will friends of Jesus who know his Father's will ask? Things in line with his will! We will ask that, in spite of our sinful nature, he would empower us to love one another.

*Heavenly Father, prune out my selfish, self-serving desires and enable me to love others as Jesus has loved me. Amen.*

# They Will Hate You

### John 15:18-21

*"If the world hates you, you know that it hated me first. If you were of the world, the world would love its own. However, because you are not of the world, but I have chosen you out of it, for that very reason the world hates you. Remember the saying I told you: 'A servant is not greater than his master.' If they persecuted me, they will persecute you too. If they held on to my word, they will hold on to yours as well. But they will do all these things to you on account of my name, because they do not know the one who sent me."*

Jesus stated a simple and obvious truth, yet a truth we so often fail to understand and accept.

It should not surprise us when people make fun of us because of our faith. It should not surprise us when people question our priorities (You're serving on a board at your church? *That* sounds like a lot of fun), or our schedules (You're going to church not only on Sunday but now on Wednesday too?!), or the way we use our money (You actually put more than a $5 bill in the plate? You actually write out $100 checks each week just to flush them down the bottomless pit of an offering plate?!). It should not surprise us when people raise eyebrows or even objections to our belief in miracles or the creation account or that Jesus' body and blood are truly present with the bread and wine in Holy Communion. It should not surprise us when people call us naïve or make fun of our belief in a God of grace, love, and forgiveness.

It should not surprise us when people hate or resent us because of Christ, because they hated and resented Christ when he came in the flesh.

Today Jesus actually tells us to take comfort in the fact that the world hates us because of him. Because if the world is hating us because of him, then it must be clear to the world that we are not simply connected to him, but we also love him.

*Lord Jesus, in the midst of hate, let me be a beacon of love—not only my love for you but, more important, your love for the world. Amen.*

---

## No Excuses

### John 15:22-25

*"If I had not come and spoken to them, they would have no sin. But now they have no excuse for their sin. The one who hates me also hates my Father. If I had not done the works among them that no one else did, they would not be guilty of sin. But now they have seen and hated both me and my Father. This was to fulfill the word which is written in their Law: 'They hated me for no reason.' "*

The religious leaders of Jesus' day were without excuse. God had come to them in human flesh. Jesus had spoken with them. He had taught with authority. He had given them testimony after testimony and witness after witness as to his identity (John the Baptist, his heavenly Father, the fulfillment of Scripture, his own Word). He had performed amazing miracles to confirm and back up his message and identity. And yet, they hated him without reason; they rejected him. Now they were without excuse. Now they were guilty of sin—specifically the sin of rejecting him. Had Jesus not come to them, had he not visited with them face-to-face, had he not taught them or performed miracles in their sight, they would not be guilty of this blatant rejection of the Son of God in human flesh (to be sure, all of their other sins would have surely condemned them). But by rejecting the one man whom God had sent to save them from sin, they were also rejecting his death on the cross that atoned for their sin and the righteousness that God would have given them through faith in Jesus. Had they not rejected Jesus, they would not have been guilty of any sin.

We really have no excuses, do we? We know who Jesus is. We celebrate his birth every year. We remember his death and celebrate his resurrection every year. There is no way we would ever reject him, right? Then let's not cut ourselves off from the one thing that keeps us connected to Jesus and assures us of and even confers on us God's forgiveness, Christ's righteousness, and the Father's declaration of "not guilty"—the means of grace: the gospel in Word and sacrament. The church year is filled with opportunities to gather with fellow Christians in God's house to hear his Word, receive the Supper, and have the Holy Spirit strengthen our faith in the one whom we by nature had and would reject.

*Thank you, Jesus. Because of you, I can stand holy and blameless before you. Amen.*

## Testify

### John 15:26,27

*"When the Counselor comes, whom I will send to you from the Father—the Spirit of truth, who proceeds from the Father—he will testify about me. And you also are going to testify, because you have been with me from the beginning."*

Lest we forget, Jesus was telling his disciples all these things the night before his death. He had told them that he was leaving them. He had told them that they could not go where he was going. He had told them that he would come back. He had encouraged them to remain in him, the vine. He had made it clear to them that the world would hate them because of him. He had told them that many would reject him.

This was a lot for the disciples to digest. Were they overwhelmed? Were they confused? Only Jesus knew. Either way, he comforted them. He promised to send them the Holy Spirit, who would counsel them and sort all this out so it made sense. Jesus kept that promise on the Day of Pentecost. The Holy Spirit came in an incredibly special way and testified about Jesus. The Holy Spirit also enabled the disciples to testify about Jesus. They did that in an incredibly special way and continued to do that even in the face of persecution.

We have so many opportunities throughout the year to testify about Jesus. Just take, for example, the month of December. What are some ways, what are some opportunities, that you have every December to explain who the baby in a manger is and why God had to take on human flesh, to explain to others what Christmas is truly about? Could you invite friends and family and neighbors to come to a special church service with you and sing carols that testify about Jesus? Could you make it a point to send Christmas cards and letters that share a religious greeting? What about other times of the year? New Year's? Valentine's Day? Lent? Easter? Summer vacation? Back to school? Reformation? Thanksgiving? As the Holy Spirit testified about Jesus to the disciples and as the disciples testified to the world about Jesus, so we too in our own way can testify about our Savior throughout the year, making seasonal ties to all that God has done for us in Jesus.

*Holy Spirit, bless the proclamation of your Word throughout the year that many people may receive the comfort and peace of knowing Jesus Christ as their Savior. Amen.*

## Be Ready

### John 16:1-4

*"I have told you these things so that you will not fall away. They will put you out of the synagogues. In fact, a time is coming when anyone who murders you will think he is offering a service to God. They will do these things because they have not known the Father or me. But I have told you these things so that when their time comes, you may remember that I told them to you. I did not tell you these things from the beginning, because I was with you."*

Jesus was preparing his disciples for life after him. The next day he would die. Then he would rise from the dead. Soon after that, though, he would ascend into heaven. He would be with them, physically, no longer. Those days would be difficult. The religious leaders would put them out of the synagogue—they would excommunicate them. They would be persecuted and even killed for their faith in Jesus—and those who did the persecuting and killing would think that they were actually doing what God wanted them to do. Jesus told them these things not to scare them, not to send them into hiding, but to prepare them. When those things happened, they could look back and say, "Remember, Jesus told us this would happen." That recollection would only reaffirm their faith and make them all the more determined—all the more ready—to live and share their faith.

Jesus said that we should not feel surprised if the world hates us because of him. Why? Not to scare us, not to send us into hiding, but to prepare us. Jesus wants us to be ready to live and share our faith. He doesn't want us to be surprised when not everyone likes who we are, what we believe, or what we stand for. He wants us to be ready to give the reason for the hope we have—no matter what the situation. We need not be intimidated. We need not shy away. We need not keep silent. We are not alone. The Lord is with us. The very Lord who died and rose for us is with us. The very Lord whom we confess is with us. The very Lord who in his exaltation has all things under his feet is with us. If God is for us, who can be against us? The answer? No one.

*Lord, the darker this world gets and the darker the situations in which I find myself become, may my light of faith shine all the more brightly. Amen.*

# I Need to Go Away

## John 16:5-7

*"But now I am going away to him who sent me, and not one of you asks me, 'Where are you going?' Yet because I have told you these things, sorrow has filled your heart. Nevertheless, I am telling you the truth: It is good for you that I go away. For if I do not go away, the Counselor will not come to you. But if I go, I will send him to you."*

To reset the scene, we remind ourselves that it was Holy Thursday evening. Jesus and his disciples were on their way out to the Garden of Gethsemane. Jesus knew that the very next day he would die. Prior to his death on the cross, Jesus was in the process of offering his disciples words of encouragement, instruction, direction, and comfort. They remained confused. They knew Jesus was going away (he had told them that), but they still didn't know where.

The greater question was why. Why was Jesus going away?

Jesus would go away from them the next day—Good Friday. He would go away from them in death, but his death would pay for their sins. They needed him to go away—and so did we.

Three days later Jesus would go away from them again—on Easter Sunday. Jesus would go away from them through his resurrection that would bring them spiritual life on earth and eternal life in heaven. They needed him to go away—and so did we.

Forty days later Jesus would go away from them again—on Ascension Day. After appearing to them numerous times to assure them that he was alive, Jesus would ascend into heaven where everything would be placed under his feet, where he would rule and govern all things for their spiritual and eternal good from the right hand of his Father. They needed him to go away—and so did we.

Ten days after that Jesus sent the Holy Spirit on the Day of Pentecost, and he has been sending the Holy Spirit through Word and sacrament ever since. None of it would mean anything if Jesus hadn't gone away in death or from the tomb or back into heaven—but he did. And so we know and believe that he will come back to take us to be with him where he is.

*Continue, Jesus, to send your Holy Spirit through Word and sacrament that I may remain prepared for your eventual return in glory. Amen.*

---

## Convicted

### John 16:8-11

*"When he comes, he will convict the world about sin, about righteousness, and about judgment: about sin, because they do not believe in me; about righteousness, because I am going to the Father and you will no longer see me; about judgment, because the ruler of this world has been condemned."*

Jesus was speaking. He was telling his disciples what will happen when he sends the Holy Spirit on the Day of Pentecost. When the Holy Spirit comes, he will convict the unbelieving world in regard to three things—sin, righteousness, and judgment.

The Holy Spirit will convict the unbelieving world in regard to sin because those who refuse to believe in Jesus forfeit the free forgiveness Jesus earned for them. Their sins will condemn them because they rejected the one—the only—way through which God provides forgiveness. Those who do not have faith in Christ do not have the forgiveness of Christ. Their unforgiven sin convicts them.

The Holy Spirit will convict the unbelieving world in regard to righteousness because those who refuse to believe in Jesus forfeit the righteous life Jesus lived in their place. The very fact that Jesus returned to his heavenly Father is evidence that Jesus perfectly carried out his Father's will—which included living a perfect life of obedience in our place. Without the righteousness of Christ covering them, their own unrighteousness convicts them.

The Holy Spirit will convict the unbelieving world in regard to judgment because those who refuse to believe in Jesus forfeit their connection not only to their divine defense attorney but also their connection to the one who took their place in the defendant's chair. They forfeit the verdict of "not guilty" in Christ, the one who not only paid the eternal fine but also provided a perfect record and a clean slate on file with God. Forfeiting their connection to Jesus, they are left to stand trial on their own, their own merit and record, and pay their eternal fine themselves, just like the devil, the prince of this world. Like him, with him, they will stand condemned.

*Thank you, Jesus! Thank you for paying for my sin with your innocent death on the cross and crediting me with your perfect obedience in life. In you I am not condemned. In you I am innocent. Thank you. Amen.*

# Soon This Will All Make Sense

### John 16:12-16

*"I still have many things to tell you, but you cannot bear them now. But when he, the Spirit of truth, comes, he will guide you into all truth. For he will not speak on his own, but whatever he hears he will speak. He will also declare to you what is to come. He will glorify me, because he will take from what is mine and declare it to you. Everything the Father has is mine. This is why I said that he takes from what is mine and will declare it to you.*

*"In a little while you are not going to see me anymore, and again in a little while you will see me, because I am going away to the Father."*

If we've been able to put ourselves in the shoes of the disciples even the slightest bit over the last two chapters of John's gospel, we have to know that they were confused. Jesus kept talking about going away. When? Where? Why? How? In answer to those questions: soon (tomorrow); Calvary (the cross); to pay for your sin; in death. They did not grasp any of that, but soon it would all make sense. After his resurrection in three days, it would begin to make sense. After his ascension into heaven in 40 days, it would make even more sense. Finally, in 50 days, on the Day of Pentecost when Jesus would send the Holy Spirit in an incredibly special way, it would make complete sense.

Isn't it great that it all makes sense to us? Isn't it an amazing blessing from God that we know the when, where, why, and how of Jesus' departure? Isn't God gracious that he clued us in through his gift of faith? Isn't it comforting, now, to remember that Jesus is coming back to take us to be with him where he is—in his Father's house? Isn't it encouraging to know that the same Spirit whom Jesus gave the disciples and the same Spirit whom God gave us is the same Spirit who can make the foolishness of the cross make sense to those with whom we share it?

*Jesus, send your Holy Spirit into the hearts of all who hear your Word that they may know and believe not only the when, where, why, and how but also the who of their salvation. Amen.*

---

# Grief or Joy

### John 16:17-22

*Therefore some of his disciples asked one another, "What does he mean when he tells us, 'In a little while you are not going to see me, and again in a little while you will see me,' and 'Because I am going away to the Father'?" So they kept asking, "What does he mean by 'a little while'? We don't understand what he's saying."*

*Jesus knew that they wanted to ask him about this, so he said to them, "Are you trying to determine with one another what I meant by saying, 'In a little while you are not going to see me, and again in a little while you will see me'? Amen, Amen, I tell you: You will weep and wail, but the world will rejoice. You will become sorrowful, but your sorrow will turn to joy. A woman giving birth has pain, because her time has come. But when she has delivered the child, she no longer remembers the anguish, because of her joy that a person has been born into the world.*

"So you also have sorrow now. But I will see you again. Your heart will rejoice, and no one will take your joy away from you."

The disciples were still scratching their heads. None of what Jesus was saying was making sense—though they did have his promise that soon the Holy Spirit would explain everything to them.

Looking back, we can know exactly what Jesus meant. Jesus would die, rise, and ascend into heaven. Jesus' death would cause his disciples to weep and mourn, but it would bring joy to his enemies and the unbelieving world. Three days later, the tables would be turned. Jesus' resurrection would bring joy to his disciples, but it would cause his enemies and the unbelieving world to weep and mourn.

In just a few short days, the disciples would be able to look back at these words of Jesus—"Now is your time of grief, but I will see you again and you will rejoice, and no one will take away your joy"—and have them make total sense.

We experience all kinds of grief in this world—none greater than the death of someone close to us. But just as it did on Easter Sunday for the disciples, so it does for us today. Jesus' resurrection will always turn our grief into joy because we know that death has been swallowed up in victory and that because he lives, we also shall live.

*Holy Spirit, in times of both grief and joy, direct my eyes of faith to my living Savior and Shepherd. Turn my grief into joy. Amen.*

# Just Ask

## John 16:23,24

*"In that day you will not ask me anything. Amen,
Amen, I tell you: Whatever you ask the Father in my
name, he will give you. Until now you have not asked for
anything in my name. Ask, and you will receive, so that
your joy may be made complete."*

Jesus' conversation with his disciples the night before his
death continued—as did their confusion. The day would
come—certainly on Easter Sunday, definitely on the Day of
Pentecost—when all of their questions would be answered.
Everything would make sense. The big picture of who Jesus
is—his work as the promised Savior and his life, death, and resurrection—would finally be clear as day. And yet, at that time,
when things finally made sense, Jesus would no longer be with
them, physically. If a question ever did arise after Pentecost, no
longer could they just turn to Jesus and ask him—"In that day
you will no longer ask me anything." Rather, they would ask the
Father. They would ask the Father in Jesus' name. They would,
quite simply, pray. And the Father, quite simply, would answer
their prayers.

Notice that Jesus didn't say, "Ask for anything." He said, "[Ask]
for anything in my name." The difference? When we pray in Jesus'
name, we are praying from a heart of faith. When we pray in
Jesus' name, we will ask according to his will. When we pray in
Jesus' name, we will focus on spiritual needs rather than material
wants. When we pray in Jesus' name, we will trust that God will
answer in a way and at a time that is best for us—we won't be
locked into our way and time. It is a very true statement and a
very real promise when Jesus tells us to ask for anything in his
name and that we will receive it. The thing to keep in mind is

not that God will need to start adjusting his answers but that, perhaps, we may need to start adjusting our prayers.

*Jesus, make my joy complete. Help me not only to receive but also to start asking for everything I need, everything those close to me need, and everything the world needs in order to have a right relationship with you. Amen.*

---

# A Direct Line to God

### John 16:25-28

*"I have told you these things using figurative language. A time is coming when I will no longer speak to you using figurative language, but I will tell you plainly about the Father. In that day you will ask in my name, and I am not telling you that I will make requests of the Father on your behalf. For the Father himself loves you, because you have loved me and have believed that I came from God. I came from the Father and have come into the world. Now I am going to leave the world and go to the Father."*

How much does God the Father love us? He has given us the right to go directly to him with any concern, problem, or request we may have. We have direct access to God the Father through Jesus—or, perhaps more accurate, because of Jesus. Because Jesus perfectly carried out God's plan of salvation, because Jesus lived and died and rose, and because Jesus returned victoriously to God the Father, we can ask the Father anything.

How much does God the Father love us? He loved us enough to send his own Son into the world to be our Savior. Had he not done that, not only could we not approach God the Father in prayer, but we would also be condemned in our unbelief and sin. The Father rescued us. He saved us from eternal condemnation by condemning his Son in our place. He saved us from death by having Jesus die in our place. He saved us from unbelief by sending the Holy Spirit into our hearts with his gift of faith. God the Father brought us into his family, and now we have not only the privilege but also the right to call him Abba, Father.

*Heavenly Father, I simply thank you for the right and privilege you have given me in Jesus to approach you in prayer. I know by nature I would have no such right—or even the desire—to pray to you. Now I have not only the right to pray but also your promise to answer. Thank you. Amen.*

---

## Take Heart

### John 16:29-33

*"Yes!" his disciples said. "Now you are speaking plainly and not using figurative language. Now we know that you know everything and do not need to have anyone ask you anything. For this reason we believe that you came from God."*

*Jesus answered them, "Now do you believe? Listen, a time is coming, in fact it is here, when you will be scattered, everyone to his own home. You will leave me all alone. Yet I am not going to be alone, because the Father is with me. I have told you these things, so that you may have peace in me. In this world you are going to have trouble. But be courageous! I have overcome the world."*

Things were beginning to make sense—in general. The disciples finally understood that Jesus had come from the Father and now was returning to the Father. But, specifically, they had no idea how the next three days would play out—the betrayal, the arrest, the trials, the suffering, the crucifixion, the death, and the resurrection. But, nonetheless, they believed. And yet their faith would be tested—in just a few short hours that faith would be put to the test—and each of them would fail. All of them would run; they would leave Jesus alone as they scattered in fear. But even in this warning, Jesus offered peace—he assured them of his ultimate victory (even though at the time they couldn't even picture the battle that would take place on the cross).

Doesn't Jesus offer us the same peace-filled warning? "In this world you are going to have trouble. But be courageous! I have overcome the world." Satan and this sin-filled world—even our own sinful nature—will put our faith to the test. But even when we fail those tests, we have the comfort that Jesus did not fail; we have the assurance of his victory; we have the comfort of his peace that comes through forgiveness. No matter what the world throws at us, no matter what trouble we experience in this world, nothing can rob us of the peace we have with and through and in Jesus.

*Through every trial and hardship, Lord, strengthen me and my faith; assure me that, as the Father was with you in your hour of trial, you are with me always. Amen.*

---

# Glory Be to Jesus

### John 17:1-5

*After Jesus had spoken these things, he looked up to heaven and said, "Father, the time has come. Glorify your Son so that your Son may glorify you. For you gave him authority over all flesh, so that he may give eternal life to all those you have given him. This is eternal life: that they may know you, the only true God, and Jesus Christ, whom you sent. I have glorified you on earth by finishing the work you gave me to do. Now, Father, glorify me at your own side with the glory I had at your side before the world existed."*

Today we begin reading John chapter 17 and our look at what has been called Jesus' High Priestly Prayer. In this chapter we will hear Jesus pray for himself and the work he was about to do; for his disciples, knowing that he would leave them behind; and finally for you and me and everyone who will believe in him. The prayer was spoken on Holy Thursday evening, just before Jesus and the disciples headed out to the Garden of Gethsemane.

The time had come for Jesus to walk the final steps to Calvary; the time had come for Jesus to suffer and die for the sins of the world. Everything that God had planned in eternity was about to be fulfilled in time—in Jesus. When Jesus prayed, "Glorify your Son that your Son may glorify you," he was asking his heavenly Father to bless the work he was about to do—his suffering, death, and resurrection—so that the Father may receive honor and praise. And how could he not receive honor and praise? Why would he not glorify his Son? Eternal life was at stake. Eternal life was about to be won. With God's blessings and through Jesus' victory, eternal life can now come to all who believe in him.

God did glorify his Son. God did bless Jesus' work of redemption. God did grant him success. God does give eternal life to all who believe in him. Want proof? Just as Jesus had asked, God the Father restored Jesus Christ to the glory he had before the world began. He did this through his resurrection and his ascension back into heaven, where he now sits at the right hand of God the Father, where he rules all things for our spiritual and eternal good, and where he constantly speaks to the Father in our defense.

*Thank you, heavenly Father, for answering your Son's prayer the night before his death. May all I do and say bring glory to you and my Savior. Amen.*

---

## Protect Them

### John 17:6-12

*"I revealed your name to the men you gave me out of the world. They were yours; you gave them to me, and they have held on to your word. Now they know that everything you have given me comes from you. For I gave them the words you gave me, and they received them. They learned the truth that I came from you. They believed that you sent me.*

*"I pray for them. I am not praying for the world, but for those you have given me, because they are yours. All that is mine is yours, and what is yours is mine. And I am glorified in them. I am no longer going to be in the world, but they are still in the world, and I am coming to you. Holy Father, protect them by your name, which*

*you gave me, so that they may be one as we are one.*
*While I was with them, I kept those you gave me safe*
*in your name. I protected them and not one of them*
*was destroyed, except the son of destruction, so that the*
*Scripture might be fulfilled."*

Jesus continued his High Priestly Prayer.

It was the night before his death—think of everything that had happened in the last three years; think of everything that would happen in the next three days.

Jesus was thankful that his heavenly Father had blessed his time with these disciples. He had blessed his Word. He had brought these men to faith in him. They knew and believed in him as their Savior. He wanted nothing to destroy that, nothing to jeopardize that. And so he prayed that they would be kept in their faith.

Jesus knew the days ahead would be extremely difficult. His disciples would see him betrayed and killed. They needed protection, comfort, and assurance. So Jesus—who had been with them the past three years to protect, comfort, and assure them and knew that he would be dead soon—asked his heavenly Father to be with them. Jesus also prayed that when he rose and ascended—when he was physically, visibly, with them no longer—his heavenly Father would continue to bless them.

With everything that was about to happen to him—and make no mistake—Jesus knew all about the betrayal, the trials, the abuse, the suffering, and the crucifixion. He knew all about the hell (literally) he was about to suffer—and his thoughts are on whom? Not on himself but on his disciples. Wow!

This is the same Jesus who is there to protect, comfort, and assure you in every doubt, need, and situation.

*Lord Jesus, let me never forget that you always remember me.*
*Amen.*

## Sanctify Them

### John 17:13-19

*"But now I am coming to you, and I am saying these things in the world, so that they may be filled with my joy. I have given them your word. The world hated them, because they are not of the world, just as I am not of the world. I am not asking that you take them out of the world, but that you protect them from the Evil One. They are not of the world, just as I am not of the world.*

*"Sanctify them by the truth. Your word is truth. As you sent me into the world, I also sent them into the world. I sanctify myself for them, so they also may be sanctified by the truth."*

Jesus' High Priestly Prayer the night before his death continued. Still in the middle section of his prayer, Jesus was praying for his disciples. His prayer was that God would sanctify them.

The word sanctify literally means "to make holy" or "to set apart." God answered this prayer of Jesus in two ways. First and foremost, God made these disciples holy through faith in Jesus. The truth of God's Word worked a faith in their hearts that received not only God's forgiveness but also Christ's holiness. Through faith, they were holy in the eyes of God, but God had also sanctified them—set them apart—in the world. God had set them apart from the unbelieving world to live holy lives—to live and share their faith.

Standing holy before God. Living holy lives in the world.

Dear Christian, that's you; that's me. God has sanctified us. Through faith in Jesus, we are holy in the eyes of God—his innocence covers our guilt, his obedience covers our disobedience, and his holiness covers our sinfulness. Empowered and guided by his Word, we now live our faith—and we now share our faith—in the world.

*Sanctify many more, Lord, through your Word of Truth that they may stand holy and blameless before you in Christ and may live holy and blameless lives in the world. Amen.*

---

## One With Him

### John 17:20-23

*"I am praying not only for them, but also for those who believe in me through their message. May they all be one, as you, Father, are in me and I am in you. May they also be one in us, so that the world may believe that you sent me. I have given them the glory you gave me, so that they may be one, as we are one: I in them, and you in me. May they become completely one, so that the world may know that you sent me and loved them even as you loved me."*

Jesus' High Priestly Prayer continued. This time, the night before his death, his prayer was for you and me.

The Savior who knew that Judas was about to betray him, the Savior who knew that the trials ahead of him would not be fair, the Savior who knew that he would suffer pain and humiliation and all kinds of hurt, the Savior who knew that by this time the next day he would have suffered an eternity's worth of hell on the cross and that he would be dead had enough love and compassion and concern in his heart that his thoughts turned from himself and his disciples to us.

He prayed that we would be one.

He prayed that he would be in us.

He prayed that we would be in him.

He prayed that we would believe in him.

In him, we are one. In him, we are glorified. In him, we are loved.

*Lord Jesus Christ, remain in me that I may remain in you. Amen.*

---

# Amen. Yes, It Shall Be So

### John 17:24-26

*"Father, I want those you have given me to be with me where I am so that they may see my glory—the glory you gave me because you loved me before the world's foundation. Righteous Father, the world did not know you, but I knew you, and these men knew that you sent me. I made your name known to them and will continue to make it known, so that the love you have for me may be in them and that I may be in them."*

Jesus brought his High Priestly Prayer to a close. He prayed for himself. He prayed for his disciples. He prayed for us. He brought his prayer to a close by simply asking his heavenly Father to advance and accomplish his eternal plan of salvation—a plan that wants all people to be saved, that is, to come to a knowledge of the truth. Jesus is that truth—as well as the way and the life. The truth is that Jesus is true God and true man. The truth is that Jesus was our substitute in life. The truth is that Jesus was our substitute in death. The truth is that Jesus defeated sin, death, and the devil; his resurrection assures us of that. God has brought us to faith in Jesus, the truth. We know it. We believe it. We trust it. We receive it.

And so, everything Jesus asked of his heavenly Father, his heavenly Father granted. Think of what that means in light of these closing statements of Jesus! He wanted us to see him in his glory—we will see him in his glory. Let us end his High Priestly Prayer with a resounding "Amen. Yes, it shall be so!"

*You are in me, dear Jesus. You made yourself known to me and made your home in my heart. Thankful for the eternal glory of heaven that awaits me, help me give you glory and honor and praise in all I do. Amen.*

---

# Betrayal

### John 18:1-3

*After saying these things, Jesus went out with his disciples across the Kidron Valley, where there was a garden. He and his disciples went into it.*

*Now Judas, who was betraying him, also knew the place, because Jesus often met there with his disciples. So Judas took the company of soldiers and some guards from the chief priests and the Pharisees, and came there with lanterns, torches, and weapons.*

The love of money is a root of all kinds of evil—so says Scripture. And it's true. Just look at what Judas' love of money led him to do—betray his Lord for 30 pieces of silver. It's more than that though, isn't it? Judas did more than betray Jesus; he threw away his faith, his salvation, heaven—all for the love of money. And his love of money brought evil of the greatest kind—torches, lanterns, weapons, clubs, spears, and, ultimately, torture, crucifixion, and death.

Some people, eager for money, have wandered from the faith—so says Scripture. That was true of Judas. May it never be true of us! The warning is sounded. Jesus reminds us, "What good is it for a man to gain the whole world and yet forfeit his soul?" (Mark 8:36). Our repentant prayer includes asking God to forgive our selfish, greedy desires, but we also ask God to keep our eyes fixed on things above, not on earthly things.

He will.

God used this evil for good. He used this betrayal to put in motion the very death that would pay for our sins.

*Forgive me, Lord, for thinking and acting as though my life revolved around money—worried when there's not enough and self-reliant when I have an abundance. Strengthen me in my faith. Keep me in faith until you call me home to the eternal mansion Jesus purchased for me on the cross. Amen.*

# I Am He

### John 18:4-9

*Jesus, knowing everything that was going to happen to him, went out and asked them, "Who are you looking for?"*

*"Jesus the Nazarene," they replied.*

*"I am he," Jesus told them.*

*Judas, the betrayer, was standing with them. When Jesus told them, "I am he," they backed away and fell to the ground.*

*Then Jesus asked them again, "Who are you looking for?"*

*"Jesus the Nazarene," they said.*

*"I told you that I am he," Jesus replied. "So if you are looking for me, let these men go." This was to fulfill the statement he had spoken: "I did not lose any of those you have given me."*

How can we read the first ten words of this account and not say "Wow!"? Jesus knew all that was going to happen to him. He didn't run, he didn't hide, he didn't avoid, he didn't lie, and he didn't resist. He said, "I am he."

Those words set everything in motion—the arrest, the trials, the taunts, the jeers, the abuse, the suffering, the condemnation, the sentencing, the crucifixion, the abandonment by his Father, and his death. And he knew it. Yet he still said, "I am he."

He was more than Jesus of Nazareth—he was the Savior of the world, the Passover Lamb, the sacrifice, the substitute. And he didn't back away from it. He faced it all, head on, and he did it for you; he did it for me.

*Jesus, you are my Savior. Thank you for your honesty in the garden. Thank you for being you. Amen.*

# I Commend You

### John 18:10,11

*Then Simon Peter, who had a sword, drew it, struck the high priest's servant, and cut off his right ear. The servant's name was Malchus.*

*So Jesus said to Peter, "Put your sword into its sheath. Shall I not drink the cup my Father has given me?"*

Do we commend Peter for his courage—willing to take on a group of men armed with clubs and swords?

Do we commend Peter for his loyalty—"You'll take this man over my dead body!"?

Do we commend Peter for wanting to do something—anything—to prevent this arrest?

Do we commend Peter for his quick thinking—"Someone has to put a stop to this!"?

Jesus did none of that. Jesus rebuked Peter. Peter, once again, hadn't seen the big picture. Jesus had to be arrested. He had to be taken away. Nothing and no one could stand in the way of that. This was God the Father's plan, and Jesus, once again, demonstrated that he was bound and determined to carry out that plan—to drink this cup of suffering.

And so we commend Jesus for his courage. He was willing to take on God's wrath and punishment.

We commend Jesus for his loyalty. God would save us because of his sacrifice for us.

We commend Jesus for wanting to do something—everything—to free us from the captivity of sin and death.

We commend Jesus for his quick thinking that, when he saw Peter's sword as a roadblock to our salvation, told Peter to put his sword away.

*Jesus, you saw the big picture; you are the big picture. Thank you for your courage and loyalty in the garden. Thank you for drinking the cup of suffering—my cup—the Father gave you to drink. Amen.*

---

# One for All

### John 18:12-14

*Then the company of soldiers, their commander, and the Jewish guards arrested Jesus and bound him. First they led him to Annas, because he was father-in-law to Caiaphas, who was the high priest that year. Now it was Caiaphas who had advised the Jews, "It is better that one man die for the people."*

It had been 15 years since Annas had officially served as high priest (he had been deposed by the Roman government). In spite of that, the people still called him the high priest—not unlike the way we continue to call a former president of the United States "President." The religious leaders still respected him, and he continued to influence the Jewish high court—the Sanhedrin. He too wanted to get rid of this Jesus. And yet, he was not the official high priest. So why did the soldiers take Jesus to him and not straight to Caiaphas?

It was late. This pretrial hearing gave Caiaphas and the other members of the Sanhedrin time to assemble the entire court. Men had to be woken up. They had to be brought to the courtroom. They had to round up the false witnesses. And yet, they had to keep this all quiet—which raises another interesting point.

According to Jewish law, a man was not to be tried and convicted on the same day he was arrested. That law didn't seem to bother them, nor did the law stating that trials were not to take place at night—only during the day. Annas and Caiaphas and the rest of their crooked court needed the cover of darkness and the rush of expediency to carry out their plot—that one would die for all, as Caiaphas so unwittingly had prophesied (John 11:50).

That was not their plot. In a much greater way, it was God's plan. It was God's plan that one—his own Son—would be the atoning sacrifice for the sins of the whole world. Jesus died on the cross so we won't have to die eternally in hell. Jesus rose from the dead on Easter Sunday so that we can rise from the dead on the Last Day.

*Your plan of salvation is no secret, though it does need to be explained and shared. Equip and empower me to be your witness in the world, Lord. Amen.*

---

# I Am Not

### John 18:15-18

*Simon Peter and another disciple kept following Jesus. That disciple was known to the high priest, so he went into the high priest's courtyard with Jesus. But Peter stood outside by the door. So the other disciple, the one known to the high priest, went out and talked to the girl watching the door and brought Peter in.*

*"You are not one of this man's disciples too, are you?" the girl at the door asked Peter.*

*"I am not!" he said.*

*The servants and guards were standing around a fire of coals that they had made because it was cold. While they warmed themselves, Peter was standing with them, warming himself too.*

When Jesus was arrested, all of the disciples fled. Terrified, they ran. To save their own skin, they deserted Jesus. At some point, two of those disciples turned around. Curious, nervous, interested, anxious, or confused—either way, they wanted to see what was going to happen to Jesus. The two disciples who turned around? Peter we know for sure; the other, most likely, was John.

John had the in. He knew Annas. He was allowed to enter. He even made it possible for Peter to enter. Great, we think. At least not all of Jesus' disciples deserted him. Wrong. Sadly, wrong. Peter's words reveal a greater abandonment than the abandonment that the legs of the others had revealed when they fled. Peter, when put on the spot by a girl on duty at the door, lied. He denied being one of Jesus' disciples. The sword-bearer just a short while ago was now intimidated by a young girl? The vocal spokesperson of the Twelve was now content just to blend in with the others around the fire? We know all too well what Peter was doing and why he was doing it. Our flesh is just as intimidated, just as fear-filled, and just as willing to lie and deny all allegiance to Jesus.

See the love of Jesus! He did not deny us. He did not lie to save his own skin when put under oath. He did not turn and run from the suffering, death, and hell that awaited him. He stood strong. He never looked back. He was determined to pay for Peter's sins of dishonesty and denial as well as our sins of trying to blend in with the crowd and hiding our faith in an effort to avoid ridicule and being made fun of. And he did pay for them. On the cross. With his blood. By his death. He forgave Peter and he forgives us.

*Jesus, empower me to boldly live and share my faith and pledge my allegiance to you in any and every situation. Amen.*

# The Pretrial

### John 18:19-24

*The high priest questioned Jesus about his disciples and his teaching.*

*Jesus answered him, "I have spoken openly to the world. I always taught in a synagogue or at the temple, where all the Jews gather. I said nothing in secret. Why are you questioning me? Ask those who heard what I told them. Look, they know what I said."*

*When he said this, one of the guards standing there hit Jesus in the face. "Is that how you answer the high priest?" he demanded.*

*"If I said something wrong," Jesus answered, "testify about what was wrong. But if I was right, why did you hit me?"*

*Then Annas sent him bound to Caiaphas the high priest.*

And so it began . . .

Jesus was put on trial, but he had committed no crime.

Jesus was questioned about his teaching, but he had said nothing in secret.

Jesus was slapped in the face, but he had done nothing wrong.

Annas was getting nowhere with Jesus. He hadn't been able to dig up any dirt on him. He hadn't been able to find any incriminating evidence against him, but perhaps this pretrial had served its purpose. Perhaps Caiaphas had been given enough time to call together enough members of the Sanhedrin—members who would go along with their plot to get rid of Jesus—at this late hour.

But this pretrial served a greater purpose than that. It had given Jesus the opportunity to testify to the truth, explain that he had said nothing in secret, and point out that everything he had taught was in line with the Word of God. This pretrial put Jesus and his innocence on display, but it also, with its trick questions and unjust slaps to the face and abusive treatment, set the stage for the other three trials Jesus was about to face—before Caiaphas, before Pilate, and before Herod.

*Through your Scriptures, Lord, you have made me wise for salvation. I thank you for the Spirit's gift of faith that opened my eyes to you and your gospel. Amen.*

---

# He Wouldn't Give Up

**John 18:25-27**

*Simon Peter continued to stand there warming himself. So they said to him, "You are not one of his disciples too, are you?"*
*He denied it, saying, "I am not!"*
*One of the servants of the high priest, a relative of the man whose ear Peter had cut off, said, "Didn't I see you with him in the garden?"*
*Peter denied it again, and just then a rooster crowed.*

Peter had already denied knowing Jesus once, but the people in that courtyard would not give up. Hardly pressing him, hardly interrogating him, hardly threatening him with any kind of force, they simply asked a question. They simply stated the truth, but Peter got defensive. Peter felt threatened. Peter was nervous and scared. Peter was driven by a perceived need to save his own skin. So he wouldn't give up—he wouldn't give up calling down curses, he wouldn't give up the lies, and he wouldn't give up the denials.

The rooster began to crow.

*Lord Jesus, forgive me for the times I have denied you. Assured of your love and forgiveness, empower me never to give up in my daily battle against my own sinful flesh. Amen.*

---

## On to Pilate

**John 18:28-32**

> *Early in the morning, the Jews led Jesus from Caiaphas to the Praetorium. They did not enter the Praetorium themselves, so that they would not become ceremonially unclean. (They wanted to be able to eat the Passover meal.) So Pilate went out to them and said, "What charge do you bring against this man?"*
>
> *They answered him, "If this man were not a criminal, we would not have handed him over to you."*
>
> *Pilate told them, "Take him yourselves and judge him according to your law."*
>
> *The Jews said, "It's not legal for us to put anyone to death." This happened so that the statement Jesus had spoken indicating what kind of death he was going to die would be fulfilled.*

The Jewish religious leaders had condemned Jesus in their unjust court. They had sentenced him to death on the basis of blasphemy, but the Jews had no authority to execute anyone. That right had been taken away by the Romans. But, interestingly enough, even if they had the right to execute someone, how would they, the Jews, have executed him? They would have stoned him to death. No Old Testament prophecy ever said that the Savior of the world would pay for the sins of the world by being stoned to death. The Old Testament Scriptures and prophecies are clear—the Savior of the world would be hung on a tree. He would be crucified. (Even Jesus had prophesied that the Son of Man would be "lifted up"—again, he would be crucified.)

Certainly, we see God's hand in the events that took place late Holy Thursday evening and early Good Friday morning. God had arranged everything. God had planned everything. And Jesus was willing to carry it all out. He was willing to be taken from the Jewish court to the Roman court. He was willing to be taken to Pilate who, eventually, would sentence him to death by crucifixion. See the plan, the detail, the progression, the fulfillment, the wisdom, the willingness, and the love of God that wants all—you and me—to be saved.

*Just as you had a plan for Jesus and the salvation of the world, Lord, I know you have a plan for me. Make me willing, as Jesus was, to trust, accept, and follow the plans you have for me. Amen.*

## I Am a King

### John 18:33-37

*Pilate went back into the Praetorium and summoned Jesus. He asked him, "Are you the King of the Jews?"*

*Jesus answered, "Are you saying this on your own, or did others tell you about me?"*

*Pilate answered, "Am I a Jew? Your own people and chief priests handed you over to me. What have you done?"*

*Jesus replied, "My kingdom is not of this world. If my kingdom were of this world, my servants would fight so that I would not be handed over to the Jews. But now my kingdom is not from here."*

*"You are a king then?" Pilate asked.*

*Jesus answered, "I am, as you say, a king. For this reason I was born, and for this reason I came into the world, to testify to the truth. Everyone who belongs to the truth listens to my voice."*

Jesus did not look like a king to Pilate. Pilate certainly did not treat him like a king—an enemy king, sure, but not a king whom he respected and obeyed.

Jesus was not the king for whom the Jews had hoped. He was not the king whom the Jews wanted. They wanted someone to drive out the Romans. They wanted someone who would restore the glory days of King David.

Is Jesus the King we want? So many times don't we try to run the show? So many times don't we fail to treat him with the honor and respect he deserves as our King? So many times, in our minds anyway, doesn't he fail to live up to our expectations as he fails to give us what we want?

Isn't it amazing, then, that Jesus came to be our King anyway? In spite of us? Or, better put, because of us? Jesus came to be the King we needed him to be. Jesus came to be a King who would give us the victory of sin, death, and the devil. Jesus served us as our King even though we refused to serve him as our King. It is because of his rule, his victory, and his power that we are now redeemed, restored, and forgiven members of his kingdom.

*Lord, use me and my life to serve others as I live under you in your kingdom. Amen.*

# Pilate Gave In

### John 18:38-40

*"What is truth?" Pilate said to him.*

*After he said this, he went out again to the Jews and told them, "I find no basis for a charge against him. But you have a custom that I release one prisoner to you at the Passover. So do you want me to release the King of the Jews for you?"*

*Then they shouted back, "Not this man, but Barabbas!" (Now Barabbas was a rebel.)*

Pilate cared little about the truth Jesus was trying to share with him. Apparently, Pilate cared little about truth in general. Because the truth was, Jesus was innocent. Pilate saw that. Pilate knew that. Pilate believed that. Pilate said that. He found no basis for a charge against him. "Surely they will ask for Jesus instead of this rebel, Barabbas," he thought to himself. He was wrong. The crowd demanded Barabbas, the known criminal, released. The crowd wanted Jesus, the innocent one, executed. Pilate gave in. He ignored the truth. He ignored justice. He gave in to the mob mentality.

God used Pilate's spineless back to advance his plan of salvation. God used a man who was so willing to deny the truth and so willing to give in to mob mentality to take his Son one step closer to the cross. And Jesus willingly walked that road. He willingly walked that road for us—for our denial of the truth and the spineless times we have given in to temptation, Jesus willingly walked the road to an innocent death that paid for our sins. Forgiven—you and me, forgiven in the blood and through the death of Jesus.

*Assured of your love, commitment, and forgiveness, Lord, make me strong in every hour of temptation that I may stand up under it or walk through the way out you have provided. Amen.*

# Where's the Love?

### John 19:1-6

*Then Pilate took Jesus and had him flogged. The sol-
diers also twisted together a crown of thorns and placed it
on his head. Then they threw a purple robe around him.
They kept coming to him, saying, "Hail, King of the Jews!"
And they kept hitting him in the face.*

*Pilate went outside again and said to them, "Look, I
am bringing him out to you to let you know that I find no
basis for a charge against him."*

*So Jesus came out wearing the crown of thorns and the
purple robe. Pilate said to them, "Behold the man!"*

*When the chief priests and guards saw him, they
shouted, "Crucify! Crucify!"*

*Pilate told them, "Take him yourselves and crucify
him, for I find no basis for a charge against him."*

No one showed Jesus any love on Good Friday—not the
Jewish religious leaders who wanted nothing less than his death,
not the mob who was so easily influenced and swayed, not Pilate
who wanted nothing to do with him, not the soldiers who had
too much fun abusing him. Everything about Good Friday leads
us to ask, "Where's the love?"

Where was the love? Not in the Jewish leaders, not in the
mob, not in Pilate, not in the soldiers. No, the love was in Jesus—
the one who took it all, the one who remained silent as he was
falsely accused, the one who had done nothing wrong, the one
who did not deserve any of this, the one who could have stopped
all this with the snap of his fingers, the one who was determined
to drink the last drop of the cup of suffering our sins had poured
for him. The love was in—and remains in—Jesus, who came to
suffer not just at the hands of people but at the hand of God.

The love was in Jesus, who would endure a far greater pain than a slap, a whip, a crown, or a taunt. The love was in Jesus, who endured hell in our place.

*I don't know how you could have loved me, Jesus. There was certainly nothing lovable about me, but you did love me. You showed me the full extent of your love by allowing yourself to be punished in my place. You, quite literally, loved me to death. Help me to show my love for you by showing love to others. Amen.*

## Who's in Control Here?

**John 19:7-11**

> The Jews answered him, "We have a law, and according to that law he ought to die, because he claimed to be the Son of God."
> When Pilate heard this statement, he was even more afraid. He went back inside the palace again and asked Jesus, "Where are you from?"
> But Jesus gave him no answer.
> So Pilate asked him, "Are you not talking to me? Don't you know that I have the authority to release you or to crucify you?"
> Jesus answered, "You would have no authority over me at all if it had not been given to you from above. Therefore the one who handed me over to you has the greater sin."

The Jews thought they were in control of this situation. They thought they could control and manipulate Pilate. They threw religious laws at him that he didn't understand or even care about. They threw at him threats of following only Caesar, not this man who claimed to be their king. They threw out loaded words like "Son of God" hoping that Pilate would cave.

Pilate thought he was in charge—at least he knew he needed to take charge. He was the Roman governor. He wasn't about to be manipulated by these Jews. He certainly didn't want a bad report to get back to Caesar. He talked tough to this weak, silent, and submissive person in front of him. He wielded his authority as he told Jesus that his fate was in the palm of Pilate's hand—to set him free or crucify him.

But who, really, was in charge of this situation? Not the Jews. Not Pilate. But Jesus. He told Pilate as much. He told Pilate that he had no authority except that which his Father had given him. Nothing was going to happen to Jesus unless he allowed it to happen. Nothing was going to take place without his approval or permission. The arrest, the trial, the sentencing, the punishment—all of these were what Jesus wanted to happen. And so, all of them happened. Who was in control? The Savior of the world.

*Jesus, your power certainly is made perfect in weakness. Though always in control, you were weak. Your weakness was stronger than human strength. And through it all, you paid for my sins. Thank you. Amen.*

---

## Shall I Crucify Your King?

### John 19:12-16

*From then on Pilate tried to release Jesus. But the Jews shouted, "If you let this man go, you are no friend of Caesar! Anyone who claims to be a king opposes Caesar!"*

*When Pilate heard these words, he brought Jesus out-*
*side. He sat down on the judge's seat at a place called the*
*Stone Pavement, or Gabbatha in Aramaic. It was about*
*the sixth hour on the Preparation Day for the Passover.*
*Pilate said to the Jews, "Here is your king!"*

*They shouted, "Away with him! Away with him!*
*Crucify him!"*

*Pilate said to them, "Should I crucify your king?"*

*"We have no king but Caesar!" the chief priests*
*answered.*

*So then Pilate handed Jesus over to them to be*
*crucified.*

*So they took Jesus away.*

Pilate was getting nowhere. He had tried several times to
set Jesus free. He told the Jews that they should take Jesus and
judge him. It didn't work. He sent him to Herod. It didn't work.
He gave the Jews a choice, Jesus or Barabbas. It didn't work. He
tried to whip, beat, and bloody him to the point that the people
would feel sorry for him. It didn't work.

The Jews kept shouting. They kept insisting. They kept
demanding. They wanted Jesus executed. They wanted Jesus
crucified. They wanted Jesus killed.

Pilate didn't get it. He didn't understand. He knew enough
about Jesus to know that he was innocent. He knew enough
about Jesus to know that he wasn't a threat. He knew enough
about Jesus that, at least at times, he was hailed, honored, and
adored by the people—even as their king. "Shall I crucify your
king?" he asked. We know their answer. What about ours? What
about our answer? If we understand God's plan of salvation and
believe, as we heard in the previous verses, that Jesus was in
complete control of all of these events, then we already know
the answer—hard as it is to say. Yes, crucify our King. That was

God's plan. That is our salvation. We say it not with an angry heart but with a sad heart. We say it not in condescension but in humility. We say it not in spite but in faith. Pilate did not crucify our King. God the Father did. He did it, yes, because of our sin, but he also did it because he loves us and wanted to save us.

*Jesus, I am humbled by your obedience and love. I am amazed at your willingness to suffer the punishment I deserved. I cannot express my gratitude enough for what you did for me, though I pray that you would help me in that effort. Amen.*

# The Place of Death

### John 19:17,18

*Carrying his own cross, he went out to what is called the Place of a Skull, which in Aramaic is called Golgotha. There they crucified him with two others, one on each side, and Jesus in the middle.*

Simple. Clear. To the point.
Historical. Factual. Real.
The judgment and sentencing had been made. Now it needed to be carried out.

Typically, four soldiers would have taken charge of the men who were to be crucified.

Typically, the criminal was forced to carry the piece of wood that would kill him. Most likely, this was only the cross beam and not the entire cross.

The Place of a Skull. Golgotha. Calvary. All one and the same place. It was called the Place of a Skull for one of two reasons:

either there was a rock formation near there that resembled a human skull or there were a number of human skulls that would have littered a nearby open pit and grave for criminals whose bodies were never claimed by family or friends.

Jesus was not alone—two other criminals were crucified with him. And yet, in just a short time, he would be very alone—forsaken and abandoned by his heavenly Father as he endured our punishment.

*Thank you for making the place of your death the place that would give me life. Amen.*

---

## No One Wanted Any Part of Him

### John 19:19-22

*Pilate also had a notice written and fastened on the cross. It read, "Jesus the Nazarene, the King of the Jews."*

*Many of the Jews read this notice because the place where Jesus was crucified was near the city, and it was written in Aramaic, Latin, and Greek.*

*So the chief priests of the Jews said to Pilate, "Do not write, 'The King of the Jews,' but that 'this man said, "I am the King of the Jews."'"*

*Pilate answered, "What I have written, I have written."*

The Jewish chief priests protested when they saw Pilate's trilingual sign above Jesus' cross—"Jesus the Nazarene, the King of the Jews." Jesus was not their king! They wanted no part of him. They wanted no connection to him, nor did they want anyone else to think that this was their king.

Pilate made it clear, by posting this sign, that he would not tolerate any threat to his rule, his jurisdiction, or Rome's authority. His sign sent that message loud and clear to all who saw it—no matter what language they spoke or read—"We will not tolerate insurrection; claim to be a king and this is what you'll get."

No one wanted any part of Jesus on Good Friday. Even God the Father abandoned Jesus on the cross. Of course, he had to. Jesus was covered with our sin. God the Father forsook Jesus so he wouldn't have to forsake us. God the Father punished Jesus on the cross (a punishment which included this abandonment—and so much more, the sufferings of hell itself) so that he would not have to punish us.

No one wanted any part of Jesus on Good Friday, but Jesus wanted us. He wanted us to be forgiven, he wanted us to be redeemed, he wanted us to be his brothers and sisters in faith, and he wanted us to be with him in heaven. Mission accomplished!

*Greater love cannot be shown than this, Jesus, that while we were still sinners, you died for us. Amen.*

---

## Why Did They Do That?

**John 19:23,24**

*When the soldiers crucified Jesus, they took his clothes and divided them into four parts, one part for each soldier. They also took his tunic, which was seamless, woven in one piece from top to bottom. So they said to one another, "Let's not tear it. Instead, let's cast lots to see who gets it." This was so that the Scripture might be fulfilled which says: "They divided my garments among them and cast lots for my clothing." So the soldiers did these things.*

Perhaps sometime today you can read Psalm 22. Psalm 22, in amazing prophetic detail, describes the suffering of Jesus—suffering fulfilled here in John chapter 19 at the hands of these Roman soldiers.

This was just another day at the office for these soldiers. They had been here before and would be here again. They had become desensitized to the brutal torture they were paid to inflict on convicted criminals. Some have commented that these Roman soldiers actually enjoyed inflicting this pain. One of the perks, one of the fringe benefits, of being the soldiers who crucified convicted criminals was to divide the spoils—to keep for themselves whatever clothing or other articles the criminal had on his person. They divided Jesus' garments among them, but they did not want to tear his undergarment—it was too nice, seamless, woven in one piece from top to bottom. They cast lots to see who would get it.

Aside from the fact that all of Jesus' clothing had to be a stained, bloody mess (one wonders why they would even want such things), there is a greater reason why they divided Jesus' garments among them and why they cast lots for his clothing. The reason? To fulfill Scripture. For Jesus to be the perfect, prophesied Savior, he had to perfectly fulfill every prophecy about the Savior. Psalm 22 states that the one who would save the world from sin would have others divide his garments and cast lots for his clothing.

Does that say anything to us? How can it not?! This was not some random criminal, and this was not just another day at the office for these soldiers. This was the prophesied Savior of the world—our Savior from sin—and what the soldiers did that morning supports that.

*Lord Jesus, a better question to ask than why the soldiers did what they did is to ask why you did what you did. I can never thank you enough for your love that moved you to humble yourself to save me from sin. Amen.*

---

## A Word of Care

### John 19:25-27

*Jesus' mother, his mother's sister, Mary the wife
of Clopas, and Mary Magdalene were standing near
the cross.*

*When Jesus saw his mother and the disciple whom he
loved standing nearby, he said to his mother, "Woman,
here is your son!" Then he said to the disciple, "Here is
your mother!" And from that time this disciple took her
into his own home.*

Even on the cross Jesus was a kind, caring, compassionate, and loving son. At a time when it would have been very natural to focus only on himself, Jesus focused on the mother he would leave behind. He saw to it that she would have a place to live and would be well cared for. The honor and respect that he showed his mother—not just on the cross but every day of his life—are the honor and respect credited by faith to our Fourth Commandment accounts on file with God. Through faith, Jesus' obedience is our obedience. If that weren't enough, the death he would soon die would be the payment in full for the sins we have committed—and will commit—against that very same Fourth Commandment.

One of the seven words that Jesus spoke on the cross was a word of care for his mother; through faith it's really a word of care he spoke on our behalf.

*Moved by your love and forgiveness and guided by your compassionate example, help me, Jesus, to show honor and respect and obey all who are in authority over me. Amen.*

## It Is Finished

**John 19:28-30**

> *After this, knowing that everything had now been finished, and to fulfill the Scripture, Jesus said, "I thirst."*
>
> *A jar full of sour wine was sitting there. So they put a sponge soaked in sour wine on a hyssop branch and held it to his mouth.*
>
> *When Jesus had received the sour wine, he said, "It is finished!" Then, bowing his head, he gave up his spirit.*

The one who had just drunk the cup of suffering that God the Father had asked him to drink—the cup of suffering our sins had poured for him—said, of all things, "I thirst." He no doubt was. What had he had to drink in the last 12 hours? How much fluid had his body lost in the last 6 hours? How excruciating had his crucifixion been? How dehydrated had he become? He was thirsty, of course, but his thirst served a greater purpose on Good Friday. His thirst fulfilled Scripture. His thirst fulfilled a prophecy about him. His thirst revealed that he was indeed the one whom God had promised to send to drink our cup of suffering. To be our Savior from sin, Jesus had to fulfill every one of the prophecies about the coming Messiah—even something as simple as thirst before death.

The wine vinegar hardly quenched his thirst, but it did wet his lips and vocal cords enough so that he could say that beautiful—and essential—phrase, "It is finished!" What was finished? Drinking that cup of suffering. Paying for our sins. Our redemption. All was finished. Literally, Jesus said, "Paid in full." Our sins were paid in full. We have nothing to pay God—there's nothing we could pay God—to make up for our sins. Our sins are already atoned for—completely. In Jesus we have full and free forgiveness.

*Every time I thirst, Lord, remind me of your Scripture-fulfilling thirst on the cross that assures me you are my promised Savior. Amen.*

## Not One of His Bones

### John 19:31-37

*Since it was the Preparation Day, the Jews did not want the bodies left on the crosses over the Sabbath (because that Sabbath was a particularly important day). They asked Pilate to have the men's legs broken and the bodies taken away. So the soldiers came and broke the legs of the first man who was crucified with Jesus, and then those of the other man.*

*But when they came to Jesus and saw that he was already dead, they did not break his legs. Instead, one of the soldiers pierced his side with a spear. Immediately blood and water came out. The one who saw it has testified, and his testimony is true. He knows that he is telling*

*the truth, so that you also may believe. Indeed, these*
*things happened so that the Scripture would be fulfilled,*
*"Not one of his bones will be broken." Again another*
*Scripture says, "They will look at the one they pierced."*

Breaking the legs and bones of those who were crucified has-
tened death. Those who were crucified would use their legs to
push themselves upward to take the weight off their lungs so that
they could gasp for a breath of air. With their legs broken—and
suffering intense pain—no longer could they push up for such
breaths of air. Suffocation—the cause of death in crucifixion—
would come much more quickly.

Jesus' legs and bones did not need to be broken—he was
already dead at this point. Was he a wimp? Was he not as strong
as the other two who had been crucified with him? Could he
not last as long as they? Hardly. Jesus had experienced far more
abuse, pain, suffering, and blood loss than they had—even before
they got out to Calvary. But all those comparisons aside, Jesus
endured something on the cross that they did not (in fact, he
endured it for them). On the cross, God was whipping Jesus. On
the cross, Jesus was enduring the pain and suffering of hell. On
the cross, Jesus paid the wages of our sin. All this—not simply
suffocation—killed him. All was completed—he declared as
much when he said, "It is finished!" So with his last, dying breath,
he entrusted his spirit to his heavenly Father.

No broken bones. A spear in his side. A sudden flow of blood
and water. These all reinforce what we already believe. The one
who died on Good Friday was and is the promised Savior—our
promised Savior—from sin.

*Thank you for a faith, Lord, that can look on you as the one who*
*was pierced for my transgressions. Amen.*

# Everything Changed

### John 19:38-42

*After this, Joseph of Arimathea, who was a disciple of Jesus, but secretly for fear of the Jews, asked Pilate to let him remove Jesus' body. When Pilate gave him permission, he came and took Jesus' body away. Nicodemus, who earlier had come to Jesus at night, also came bringing a mixture of myrrh and aloes, about seventy-two pounds.*

*They took Jesus' body and bound it with linen strips along with the spices, in accord with Jewish burial customs.*

*There was a garden at the place where Jesus was crucified. And in the garden was a new tomb in which no one had ever been laid. So they laid Jesus there, because it was the Jewish Preparation Day, and the tomb was near.*

Everything changed for Joseph on Good Friday—the fear, the lack of courage, the failure to trust God. Everything changed for Joseph on Good Friday when he saw Jesus on the cross paying for his sins. Here—in front of him, above him—was his Savior who was not afraid, who did not lack courage, whose trust in God was not fickle. Here was his Savior who faced death so that he wouldn't have to. Here was his Savior who courageously and willingly threw himself under the bus of God's wrath and punishment. Here was his Savior who, though men mocked and jeered him as the Son of God, put his trust in God, committing his spirit to him with his last dying breath. Joseph looked at the cross of Christ and saw his free forgiveness. That too is where we look. With guilty consciences and penitent hearts, we look in faith to our Savior, who was lifted up so that all who believe in him may have eternal life. On the cross we see our Savior from sin. On the cross we see our forgiveness won.

Joseph hadn't taken advantage of the opportunities he had to worship Jesus while he was still alive; he wouldn't miss those opportunities now that Jesus was dead. He would worship Jesus by burying him with the honor, respect, and dignity he deserved. He would give Jesus his own tomb, a tomb cut out of rock, a tomb that had never been used, a tomb that was in a garden near Golgotha, a tomb that would bury Jesus among the rich—just as Isaiah had prophesied. But as nice as that tomb was, Jesus did not stay in that tomb. He rose from the dead. He left that fancy tomb and all those spices behind. Jesus is alive. In Jesus, we have a living Savior who defeated death. We have a living Savior whom we can worship every day. Worship is not just what we do in church; worship is what we do in life. Like Joseph and as Paul says in Romans 12:1, we offer our bodies as living sacrifices to God, holy and pleasing to him; this is our spiritual act of worship.

*Jesus, may all I do for others be an expression of my love for you. Amen.*

## Run to the Tomb

### John 20:1-9

*Early on the first day of the week, while it was still dark, Mary Magdalene went to the tomb. She saw that the stone had been taken away from the tomb. So she left and ran to Simon Peter and the other disciple, the one Jesus loved. "They have taken the Lord out of the tomb," she told them, "and we don't know where they put him!"*

*So Peter and the other disciple went out, heading for the tomb. The two were running together, but the other*

*disciple outran Peter and got to the tomb first. Bending*
*over, he saw the linen cloths lying there, yet he did*
*not go in.*

*Then Simon Peter, who was following him, arrived*
*and went into the tomb. He saw the linen cloths lying*
*there. The cloth that had been on Jesus' head was not*
*lying with the linen cloths, but was folded up in a sepa-*
*rate place by itself. Then the other disciple, who arrived*
*at the tomb first, also entered. He saw and believed.*
*(They still did not yet understand the Scripture that he*
*must rise from the dead.)*

The weekend had to be tough. Things had already begun to
spiral out of control on Thursday evening—the betrayal, the
arrest, Peter's denial, the unjust trial. Things only got darker on
Friday morning—the trials before Pilate and Herod, the abuse
of the soldiers, the walk (or crawl) out to Calvary, the crucifixion, Jesus' death. A feeling of helplessness must have consumed
Mary and the other women as they watched. Feelings of guilt
and loss must have filled Peter's heart and mind. With the stone
placed in front of the tomb late Friday afternoon and with nothing happening on Saturday, the weekend had to be tough. "Now
what?" was the question of many. Mary had plans to give Jesus
her own burial early Sunday morning, but Jesus wasn't there!
Peter and John ran to the tomb with both questions and hope.
Peter and John ran to the tomb for answers. The answer was that
Jesus was alive.

Run to the tomb! When guilt consumes, run to the tomb.
When life is tough, run to the tomb. When questions abound,
run to the tomb. When you begin to doubt, run to the tomb.
When you are weak, run to the tomb. When you are overwhelmed, run to the tomb. The answer to guilt, sin, hopelessness,
helplessness, questions, doubt, weakness, and a sense of being

overwhelmed is that Jesus is alive. He is alive to remove our sin and guilt. He is alive to help us through life, give us strength in all things, guide our paths, calm our fears, and erase our doubts. We have a living Savior! In life, run to the tomb.

*Remind me always, Jesus, that not only are you alive but you are with me always. Amen.*

---

## Saying Her Name Was All It Took

**John 20:10-18**

> *Then the disciples went back to their homes.*
> *But Mary stood outside facing the tomb, weeping. As she wept, she bent over, looking into the tomb. She saw two angels in white clothes sitting where the body of Jesus had been lying, one at the head and one at the feet. They asked her, "Woman, why are you weeping?"*
> *She told them, "Because they have taken away my Lord, and I don't know where they have laid him."*
> *After she said this, she turned around and saw Jesus standing there, though she did not know it was Jesus.*
> *Jesus said to her, "Woman, why are you weeping? Who are you looking for?"*
> *Supposing he was the gardener, she replied, "Sir, if you carried him off, tell me where you laid him, and I will get him."*
> *Jesus said to her, "Mary."*
> *She turned and replied in Aramaic, "Rabboni!" (which means, "Teacher").*

*Jesus told her, "Do not continue to cling to me, for I have not yet ascended to my Father. But go to my brothers and tell them, 'I am ascending to my Father and your Father—to my God and your God.'"*

*Mary Magdalene went and announced to the disciples, "I have seen the Lord!" She also told them the things he said to her.*

Mary was beside herself. Not only was Jesus dead but now his body was missing. She didn't know what to do. She didn't know what to think. Her world had changed dramatically over the past week. She was now desperate.

Things were about to change dramatically once again—this time for the good. She would know what to think, what to do. Desperation would turn to excitement, fear to confidence, sadness to joy, loneliness to comfort, anxiety to trust. And all it would take for things to change so dramatically would be her name, someone saying her name—not just anyone but her Lord and Savior, her living Lord and Savior, Jesus. "Mary." That was all it took. Jesus was alive and Mary's tears were gone.

Those of you who know and have sung "I Am Jesus' Little Lamb" may recall one line of the song that says that Jesus "even calls me by my name." Jesus calls us by name. He knows us. He loves us. He reaches out to us. He comforts us. He forgives us. He leads us. He guides us. He guards us. He protects us. He changes everything for us—fear to confidence, sadness to joy, loneliness to comfort, anxiety to trust. And all it took was saying our name—and his—at the font where through water and Word he put his name on us and adopted us into his family.

*You have called me into your family, Lord. You have changed my life dramatically. Help me show my love and appreciation by sharing your life-giving name with others. Amen.*

# Peace Be With You

### John 20:19-23

*On the evening of that first day of the week, the disciples were together behind locked doors because of their fear of the Jews. Jesus came, stood among them, and said to them, "Peace be with you!" After he said this, he showed them his hands and side. So the disciples rejoiced when they saw the Lord.*

*Jesus said to them again, "Peace be with you! Just as the Father has sent me, I am also sending you." After saying this, he breathed on them and said, "Receive the Holy Spirit. Whenever you forgive people's sins, they are forgiven. Whenever you do not forgive them, they are not forgiven."*

On Easter Sunday the disciples were gathered together not in joy—not to worship their risen Lord, not to proclaim his victory—but in fear behind locked doors, hoping that no one would find them. Jesus changed all that. Jesus came and stood among them—in the flesh, alive. Fear turned to joy. A gathering intent on keeping quiet became a gathering intent on shouting praises. Locked doors of protection became open doors of evangelism. Jesus changed everything. Easter changed everything. Jesus brought them—he gave them—his peace: the peace of sins forgiven, the peace of reconciliation, the peace of eternal life.

On top of that, Jesus gave them the ministry of the keys. He gave them a key that would warn those who were wrapped up in some ongoing sin; he also gave them a key that would comfort those who had become unraveled by some ongoing sin. These keys are the keys to the kingdom of heaven. They close heaven's door to those who refuse to confess their sins; they open heaven's door to those who rely on their Savior for his free forgiveness.

No more fear. No more hiding. No more locked doors. Jesus' resurrection has changed everything for us. We have peace, joy, and confidence because of his resurrection. Our lives—we—now have meaning, purpose, and direction.

*Lord, help me, in love, to make faithful use of the keys to heaven that you have entrusted to me and every member of your church. Amen.*

---

## There Is No Doubt

### John 20:24-29

> *But Thomas, one of the Twelve, the one called the Twin, was not with them when Jesus came. So the other disciples kept telling him, "We have seen the Lord!"*
> *But he said to them, "Unless I see the nail marks in his hands and put my finger into the mark of the nails, and put my hand into his side, I will never believe."*
> *After eight days, his disciples were inside again, and Thomas was with them. Though the doors were locked, Jesus came and stood among them. "Peace be with you," he said. Then he said to Thomas, "Put your finger here and look at my hands. Take your hand and put it into my side. Do not continue to doubt, but believe."*
> *Thomas answered him, "My Lord and my God!"*
> *Jesus said to him, "Because you have seen me, you have believed. Blessed are those who have not seen and yet have believed."*

Thomas had his doubts. In reality, Thomas refused to believe. He wasn't there on Easter Sunday when Jesus appeared to the other disciples. He wasn't going to believe that Jesus was alive unless he had proof—living proof—his fingers in the holes, his hand in the side. A week later, in love, Jesus appeared again. This time Thomas was there. Jesus offered the proof Thomas had selfishly demanded, proof he had had no right to demand, proof Jesus was not obligated to give Thomas but gave him anyway. Thomas never did accept Jesus' invitation to put his finger "here" or touch his side; he didn't need to; he had already stopped doubting; by grace he believed. He confessed his faith in Jesus as his Lord and God.

There is no doubt that Jesus rose from the dead. No, we haven't seen Jesus in the flesh, and yet our faith embraces him. We haven't touched him in the flesh, and yet we point to him as our living Lord and Savior. The Holy Spirit is the one who gives us this living faith in a living Savior. The Holy Spirit gets all the credit that we who have not seen and yet have believed are blessed. We are blessed with a faith that sees and receives a living Savior's blessings of forgiveness, peace, and eternal salvation.

*Jesus, how my heart yearns within me that one day I will see you with my own eyes, in the flesh, I and not another! By faith I know that you, my Redeemer, live! I look forward to that day when I will stand with you in heaven. Amen.*

# Life in His Name

### John 20:30,31

*Jesus, in the presence of his disciples, did many other miraculous signs that are not written in this book. But these are written that you may believe that Jesus is the Christ, the Son of God, and that by believing you may have life in his name.*

Why write—and read—these devotions? Why did John write—and we read—his gospel? Why did the Holy Spirit inspire men to write the 66 books that are the Bible?

So that we may believe.

So that we may believe that Jesus is the Christ.

So that we may believe that Jesus Christ lived in our place, died in our place, and rose from dead.

So that we may believe and have life in his name—eternal life in heaven.

Paul tells us in Romans that faith comes from hearing the message and the message is heard through the Word of Christ.

Today we thank the Holy Spirit for the inspired Word of God that tells us not only who we were and what we deserved but also who God is and what he freely gives. We thank the Holy Spirit for working through that inspired Word of God to create, sustain, and strengthen the saving faith in Jesus that he has given us. We ask the Holy Spirit to keep us in that Word—and in faith—until Jesus returns on the Last Day or until that day when he calls us home to life in heaven through an earthly death.

*Thank you, Holy Spirit, for the Word of God and the faith to believe it—for all who believe it shall not perish but have eternal life. Amen.*

# This Is No Fish Story

## John 21:1-14

*After this, Jesus showed himself again to the disciples at the Sea of Tiberias. This is how he showed himself: Simon Peter, Thomas (called the Twin), Nathanael from Cana in Galilee, the sons of Zebedee, and two other disciples were together. Simon Peter said to them, "I'm going fishing."*

*They replied, "We'll go with you."*

*They went out and got into the boat, but that night they caught nothing. Early in the morning, Jesus was standing on the shore, but the disciples did not know it was Jesus.*

*Jesus called to them, "Boys, don't you have any fish?"*

*"No!" they answered.*

*He told them, "Throw your net on the right side of the boat and you will find some." So they cast the net out. Then they were not able to haul it in because of the large number of fish.*

*The disciple whom Jesus loved said to Peter, "It is the Lord!" When Simon Peter heard, "It is the Lord!" he tied his outer garment around him (for he had taken it off) and jumped into the sea. But the other disciples came in the little boat, dragging the net full of fish, for they were not far from shore, about one hundred yards. When they stepped out on land, they saw some bread and a charcoal fire with fish on it. Jesus said to them, "Bring some of the fish you just caught."*

*So Simon Peter climbed aboard and hauled the net to land, full of large fish, 153 of them. Yet even with so many, the net was not torn.*

*Jesus said to them, "Come, eat breakfast."*

*None of the disciples dared ask him, "Who are you?" because they knew it was the Lord.*

*Jesus came, took the bread, and gave it to them, and also the fish. This was now the third time Jesus appeared to his disciples after he was raised from the dead.*

Fishermen have a way of exaggerating the truth. "This big" has a way of growing into "THIS BIG!" What John records for us here, however, is no fish story. The disciples, sometime after Easter, really did catch 153 large fish—and this, on just one cast of the net, came after a night of catching no fish. John was the first to see who was behind this miraculous catch of fish—"It is the Lord!" These 153 fish revealed the almighty power of the risen Lord. For the third time, Jesus assured his disciples that he had defeated death. They too would live—forever in heaven.

The risen Lord who appeared to his disciples on the shore of the Sea of Galilee is the same risen Lord who comes to us in Word and sacrament to assure us that he has defeated death and we too shall live. The risen Lord who displayed his almighty power to his disciples in this miraculous catch of fish is the same risen Lord who will return on the Last Day in a great display of power and glory to take us home to heaven. That's no tall tale. That's no fish story. That's the gospel truth.

*Lord Jesus, give me a faith that trusts in you, your almighty power, your infinite wisdom, and your loving care in all things. Amen.*

# Feed My Sheep

### John 21:15-17

*When they had eaten breakfast, Jesus asked Simon Peter, "Simon, son of John, do you love me more than these?"*

*"Yes, Lord," he said, "you know that I care about you."*

*Jesus told him, "Feed my lambs."*

*A second time Jesus asked him, "Simon, son of John, do you love me?"*

*He said, "Yes, Lord, you know that I care about you."*

*Jesus told him, "Be a shepherd for my sheep."*

*He asked him the third time, "Simon, son of John, do you care about me?"*

*Peter was grieved because Jesus asked him the third time, "Do you care about me?" He answered, "Lord, you know all things. You know that I care about you."*

*"Feed my sheep," Jesus said.*

It is no coincidence that Jesus asked Peter three times if he loved him. Three times, Peter had denied Jesus. Three times, he was able to profess his love for Jesus. Many have said, and rightly so, that after his resurrection, on the shore of the Sea of Galilee, Jesus reinstated Peter into his call as an apostle to feed and care for God's sheep. More than just this reinstatement into the public ministry, Jesus was also assuring Peter of his love and forgiveness.

Isn't it amazing that in spite of our own denials, in spite of our own sins, Jesus still calls us to feed his lambs and take care of his sheep? Granted, those calls may not be calls into the public ministry, but they are callings in life, nonetheless. Those lambs and sheep may be our own children, our grandchildren, our nieces and nephews, friends of the family, or children in the neighborhood. Moved by the love and forgiveness that Jesus has for us, we have opportunity after opportunity to share that same love and forgiveness with others. And they don't even have to be children—they can be anyone who hungers for the Bread of Life or thirsts for the living water of the gospel.

*Lord, you know all things. You know that I love you. Help me now to show that love for you as I share your Word with others. Amen.*

---

## Follow Him

### John 21:18-25

*"Amen, Amen, I tell you: When you were young, you dressed yourself and went wherever you wanted. But when you are old, you will stretch out your hands, and someone else will tie you and carry you where you do not want to go."*

*Jesus said this to indicate the kind of death by which Peter would glorify God. After saying this, he told him, "Follow me."*

*Peter turned and saw the disciple Jesus loved following them. This was the one who had leaned back against Jesus at the supper and asked, "Lord, who is going to betray you?" When Peter saw him, he asked Jesus, "Lord, what about him?"*

*"If I want him to remain until I come," Jesus answered, "what is that to you? You follow me." And so it was said among the brothers that this disciple would not die. Yet Jesus did not say that he would not die, but, "If I want him to remain until I come, what is that to you?"*

*This is the disciple who is testifying about these things and who wrote these things. We know that his testimony is true.*

*Jesus also did many other things. If every one of them were written down, I suppose the world itself would not have room for the books that would be written.*

Jesus had just reinstated Peter on the shores of the Sea of Galilee. He had called him to feed his sheep. Peter's calling as a public servant of the Word would cost him his life; Jesus told him as much. He even indicated that Peter would be crucified for his faith—"You will stretch out your hands." In spite of this, or, perhaps, because of this, Jesus encouraged Peter to follow him at all times.

John too had a life of service in the public ministry ahead of him—a long life of service ahead of him. He would follow Jesus and feed his sheep some 60 more years, even as he was exiled on the Island of Patmos where he wrote the inspired book of Revelation. John, tradition holds, was the only one of the apostles not to die a martyr's death.

What about us? Isn't the call—the encouragement—the same for us to follow Jesus? Of course it is! Come what may, we have the promise and assurance of our risen and ascended Lord that he will walk with us every step of the way as we live our faith, let our light shine, and share his Word with others.

*Lord Jesus, give me the courage and strength I need to boldly live my faith and share your Word of salvation with others. Amen.*